THE REAL ESTATE RULEBOOK

Editors: Earl Tillinghast, Regina Cornell

Cover Design: 3SIXTY Marketing Studio

Interior Design: 3SIXTY Marketing Studio

Indigo River Publishing
3 West Garden Street Ste. 352
Pensacola, FL 32502
www.indigoriverpublishing.com

Ordering Information:

Quantity sales: Special discounts are available on quantity purchases by corporations, associations, and others. For details, contact the publisher at the address above.

Orders by U.S. trade bookstores and wholesalers: Please contact the publisher at the address above.

Printed in the United States of America

Library of Congress Control Number: 2017951033
ISBN: 978-0-9990210-4-0

First Edition

With Indigo River Publishing, you can always expect great books, strong voices, and meaningful messages. Most importantly, you'll always find...words worth reading.

Table of Contents

PREFACE

Real estate has been my passion since I bought my first duplex while serving in the Navy in Jacksonville, Florida. I am now 60 years old, have gone through 3 divorces, and my net worth is somewhere over three million dollars because of real estate. Real estate investing can make ordinary people a lot of money over a lifetime. Why should you read my book? I am an ordinary middle-class female with a story to tell about how I did it. I am assuming real estate has piqued your interest because you picked up this book, so if you are interested in making money, I think my story can help you. This is not a story that involves "get rich quick" techniques; it is about long-term planning, buying houses one at a time, minimizing financial risk, and building equity.

My husband and I were a double-income no kids young couple in 1978, and his goal was to be a millionaire by the time he reached 35. We were both active duty in the Navy: I was a nurse and he had just earned his wings as a helicopter pilot. My husband George was 24 years old; I was 23. We bought an older, brick duplex, and it needed work, so we spent our free time fixing it up. This included things like scraping paint and tearing down old wallpaper: lots of paint, lots of time and elbow grease, but not that much money because we did it all ourselves. Upon completion, we moved in the downstairs and rented the upstairs unit. It was actually fun and gave me a sense of accomplishment, and the rent from the upstairs unit paid about two-thirds of our mortgage payment, which made it even better. We saved up some money and a year later bought another home, rehabbed it, moved in, and rented out our other apartment.

When my husband went on deployment for six months with the Navy, I decided that if I was going to pursue our investments in real estate, I should learn all that I could so I proceeded to take the Florida Real Estate Pre-Licensing Course as well as read other books about real estate and attended seminars. It was 1979; I was active duty in the Navy, and I decided to get my license and become a part-time realtor and investor.

REALTOR®- Has one and only one meaning: A federally registered collective membership mark which identifies a real estate professional who is a member of the NATIONAL ASSOCIATION OF REALTORS® and SUBSCRIBES TO ITS STRICT CODE OF ETHICS.

Fixed rate mortgage interest rates were about 16% but that did not stop me. I learned to make deals with assumable mortgages (before the rules changed), wrap around mortgages, adjustable rate mortgages, and owner financing. All of which are examples of "creative financing."

Assumable Mortgage- taking over the seller's mortgage

Wraparound Mortgage- a financing arrangement between buyer and seller whereby the buyer executes an installment note which **"wraps around"** an existing **mortgage** still held by the seller; more simply, it is a type of financing where the seller carries a portion of the buyer's loan

Adjustable-Rate Mortgage- the interest rate is adjusted periodically to reflect market conditions.

Owner Financing- the seller takes the role of the lender; buyer makes monthly payments directly to the seller

In 1981, we both transferred to Pensacola, Florida, where I still reside. We kept all the properties in Jacksonville but soon discovered that managing housing from six hours away while working full-time could have its challenges, so I hired my first property manager.

Fast forward to 1985, we both left the military and opened our own real estate company, with me as the broker and he the sales agent. I also had Plan B which was to stay active in PRN nursing and to affiliate with the local Navy Reserve Unit.

Life happened, and before I knew it, I was the mother of four and seven-year-old girls and getting divorced. There was a business and some property we owned that needed to be divided. I agreed to split the business and do the property management part-time, and got a job as a nurse. I took sole title to the investment property we owned in lieu of depending on child support payments, and that ended our marriage. Child support would have ended in 2004 when my youngest daughter Nicole turned 18; however, I am still collecting income from one of those properties today, and the sale of others helped buy my kids their first cars when they turned 16 and provided additional family support.

After my divorce, I remarried, and for 5 years, I devoted much of my time to my nursing job and my family which grew to three children and 2 step children, but real estate was always in the background providing me with monthly cash flow, and I was still a landlord. There was not much extra money to buy additional properties during that time, but my passion for real estate never died, and the first thing I did after getting divorced was to purchase a canal front home in the Santa Rosa Shores neighborhood in Gulf Breeze, Florida, which was a great place to raise my kids, and it turned out to be a really good investment.

In 1997, I was in the Naval Reserves and working as a nurse when I injured my neck and had to have spinal surgery. After the surgery, I was supposed to be off for four weeks medical leave, but I never went back to my nursing job. Instead, I went back full time into real estate, and I have never looked back. Today, I own and operate a very successful family business which I started in 1998 and plan to turn operations over to my children over the next several years. I have combined my personal long- and short-term investment strategies with a real estate business plan that focuses on helping others to invest for the long term, as well as providing the needed real estate sales and property management services through my company.

This book is meant to be entertaining and easy to read, full of real-life experiences, both successes and mistakes. I will give you detailed examples of how I did it and what it takes to reach financial freedom using real estate. It also will include insights from my children, who have been with me throughout the journey. I could not be where I am today without them.

Chapter 1:
Motivation and
Financial Success Principles

What follows is not a "get rich quick" scheme, but it is a sound, long term approach for success over time. No matter what your current situation in life is, building financial wealth through investing in real estate is available to you. Right now, you may feel powerless, you may not have the necessary knowledge, or money for that matter, but a great ending is possible if you believe in yourself.

Researchers have found your level of motivation is more significant in predicting success than either your IQ or ability. I have watched this play out in my life and others around me. Those that lack motivation and realistic goals quickly fall off their path to their dreams and never get back on. I hope that my story will motivate and influence you to take action, but it begins with you. Start with a passion to reach your ultimate goal: the long term motivation follows.

Most would say being rich is about having money. You can have a job and be very rich, but that money stops coming when you stop working. Financial wealth, on the other hand, is about owning assets such as stocks, businesses, or real estate that generate money for you. The definition of financial wealth is *the unearned income to finance your life mission without having to work.* Only 1% of all people make enough money from their jobs to ever truly become financially wealthy. These are people like professional athletes, actors, and top executives. Even these people should take an active role in investing their money for the future as these jobs don't last forever, and people who earn more tend to spend more, so without proper planning, they can run out of money just like you and me.

I believe a basic principle you need to learn early on in life is to live off less than you earn. You should think of your job as not only a way to pay your bills but also as a way to earn your initial investment capital. Not everyone can get 100% financing like I did on my first investment, but you can start without a lot of money—you just need to get started. And the younger you are when you start the easier it becomes, and the more wealth you can have over time.

In my case, due to working other jobs, raising three children, and marriages that ended in divorce, as well as the ups and downs of our economy, it took me longer to reach my goals; but the important thing now is not only will I have a secure retirement ahead, but I will also have a legacy to pass along to my children and grandchildren. Today, when I get up and go to work, it is not because I need a paycheck. I do it because I still love what I do and I want to help others, especially my family.

Below is a picture of my granddaughter Lily, age five; grandson Cale, age four; and baby Grace.

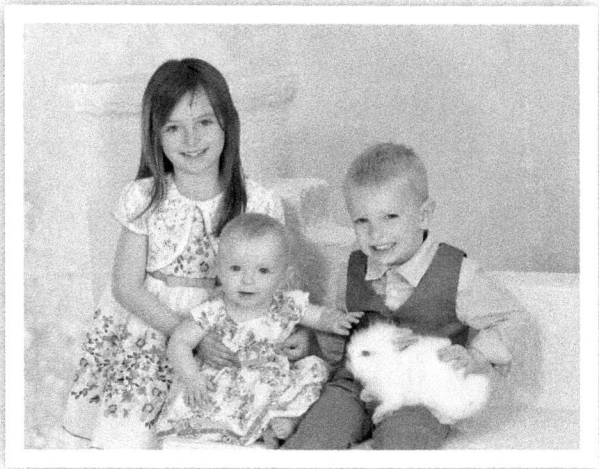

Any discussion of wealth building needs to talk about the subject of money. I was brought up in the Catholic Church as a child. A lot of Christians and Catholics use the term "God will provide," and I believe that statement is true, but I also believe that he gives us intelligence and certain other gifts, and he expects us to use them wisely. He wants us to be able to figure out how to make enough money to live and take care of our families.

I don't think of money as either good or bad; I think money gives you choices. You choose how to spend, invest, or save it. Those choices reveal your true character such as whether you are generous or greedy, honest or dishonest. Honesty, hard work, and fair dealing with others pay off in the long run.

I grew up in Wisconsin in a lower-middle-class family, the youngest of five children. My parents did not have a lot of money, but they were good, hardworking people, and they taught me the value of working, saving a little of what you earn, and owning a home. I lived in the same home for the first 18 years of my life. As a child, I was rewarded for good behavior and good grades on my report card. I found that I loved to learn, some things more than others, and I used the intelligence I was given to earn good grades. I graduated in the top of my class and earned a scholarship to Marquette University in Milwaukee, Wisconsin, where I studied nursing. I married my high school sweetheart while still in college, and joined him after graduation in Pensacola, Florida, where he was studying to become a Navy pilot, so I have him and the Navy to thank for the opportunity to live in paradise.

Honesty, hard work, and fair dealing with others pay off in the long run.

My life with my first husband was an emotional roller coaster that ended in divorce, but I have him to thank for fathering my two wonderful daughters and for leading me to enter the world of finances and real estate. He always said he would be a millionaire by the age of 35. I had never really thought about the possibility of that before, but we started to save and worked together to buy houses while we were both in the Navy. Upon getting off active duty, we opened a real estate brokerage. (See Appendix A for the requirements to open a real estate company in Florida. Each state has different requirements so check with your state if this is something you want to do.)

We also continued to invest when we could. I liked that through the MLS (Multiple Listing Services) and our clients, deals presented themselves, and we learned more about the business. I hired other people to work for the business, managed the rental of the properties we owned, and provided management services for others who needed that service. After renting them for several years, we sold the properties in Jacksonville, Florida, and took the money we made on the sales and reinvested in more properties in Pensacola, so we could more easily manage them ourselves.

Although I was sad when the marriage ended, I was left with two beautiful daughters who gave me a reason to keep on working and investing. My husband never quite reached his goal of being a millionaire before we divorced, but I knew by then that it was possible to reach that goal for myself and my girls.

One thing I had learned from being married and in business with the same person was that it was difficult to make it all work. He was a great salesperson, and he was so intelligent: he had lots of good ideas but difficulty finishing things. I was the opposite, and I learned that I had to hold things together and depend on myself. Even when I was married, I felt like a single parent when it came to dropping off and picking the kids up from daycare, doing the household chores, keeping the office open five days a week Monday through Friday, taking care of the taxes and paying the bills and on and on. It was always me that held it together, so when we divorced, I already knew that anything is possible if you have passion and the determination to carry on. I agreed on a marital settlement where he paid no child support: he got the office building and the sales business and a house to live in. I took the rentals we had accumulated during the marriage and the property management portion of the business as I knew those two things would provide me some cash flow on a monthly basis. He jumped at the chance of not having to deal with tenants and maintenance and no child support—what could be sweeter? He was interested in his new romance who was more than 15 years younger than he was. I had the kids almost all the time; he took them every other weekend. I was now the sole owner of six rental homes, the home I lived in, and one commercial building, and had $175,000 in debt.

Initially, I calculated my average monthly cash flow was around $900 a month net after paying t he loans and the taxes and insurance and set aside about 10% for maintenance. Over time that grew as I was able to work on paying off some of the debt. I was a bit nervous about raising two kids and doing this alone, so I also went back to plan B for a few years and took a job in nursing so I could continue to support my children and grow my real estate investments. It was the end of 1991; I had turned 36 years old. I was a landlord and my properties were small, older homes and one small commercial building. None of them were located in the best neighborhoods of Pensacola, but I felt it was better than the alternative which was to depend on a child support check from my ex-husband every month. I was building financial wealth, and I was not going to let a little thing like a divorce get in my way!

Mindset is very important in life. Developing the right mindset is perhaps the most important thing you can do to create success for your life in real estate or any other path you may choose. This is really not something that comes naturally, and most people have to work at it. I know I did and still do. Your mindset is easily sucked into the negativity and pessimism of others around you, especially family, friends, or coworkers you spend a lot of time with. You really need to think the right thoughts, develop the right habits and continually work on self-improvement and do not let others keep you from achieving your goals.

There are many books written on the subject of success, one I particularly like was published in 2005 called *The Success Principles* by Jack Canfield who co-created *Chicken Soup for the Soul.* Other people whose books I have read or watched and listened to their DVDs are people like Tony Robbins and John Maxwell. If you have not done this before, I hope you will start to read books, listen and watch DVDs, recite affirmations, do whatever it takes to get and keep a positive attitude and always believe in yourself: that's what it takes to succeed in life and at building wealth.

In order to build wealth using real estate, you must believe in yourself first, and second you must develop an "Investor Mindset." I only figured that one out when I was in the middle of the divorce because, before that, my husband did a lot of the thinking and he bought the properties. I just dealt with the day-to-day. My husband was in control of the big thinking. I was the caregiver or "doer." I had to move from being the one who was the doer to thinking and doing. In nursing we always had to take orders from the doctor, so I was used to that, but my divorce was the thing that put me back in control and in charge of my own future.

When I was growing up in the '60s and '70s, women were pretty much second-class citizens, and I was programmed by society to do as I was told. As an officer the military, though, I had been sent to leadership training with men to learn how to be an officer, and I slowly learned that I was capable of doing anything a man could, sometimes better. The more I learned about real estate, the more confident I became. My husband was not very receptive to my suggestions about how I thought we should do things, so we started fighting about business, and it affected his ego and our personal relationship. Be aware, if you are married, your partner's mindset can be a challenge. Try your best to include your partner in the decision-making process as disagreements over finances can derail all of your plans if you are not careful. I will admit that divorce affected my self-esteem and my mindset, and I had to work hard to overcome it.

There are actually two ways people view their financial potential. There are those who think in terms of "probability" or what is likely to be achieved based on their past history and current capabilities.

Then there are those who think in terms of "possibilities," which is more like what I can imagine. Probability thinkers are more likely to say "I can't do that;" possibility thinkers base their view of their financial future on what they imagine themselves to be capable of accomplishing. They are dreamers, and they take into account that they might have to learn new things or change their habits to reach their full potential. My advice to you is to start small and think big. It takes perseverance, but you can make it big on small deals over time. All it takes is a little time, money, and ability.

Probability thinkers are more likely to say I can't do that; possibility thinkers base their view of their financial future on what they imagine themselves to be capable of accomplishing.

You can start now by rating yourself from 1-10, with 10 being the highest, on these three things:

> → How much time do you currently have to spend on investing? You will definitely need to make a time commitment. Most people will start investing part-time. Maybe you only have a few hours a week to start, just remember small steps can result in big rewards over time. The younger you are the more your results will compound over time, and we will talk about this concept more in the next chapter.

→ How much money do you have to work with? If you don't have money yourself, you can always take on a financial partner or borrow the money. One of the best things about investing in real estate is if you don't have money you can use other people's money. You can borrow money to invest in real estate using the property as collateral.

→ What do you know about the process? You don't have to know everything. Start with what you do know and build on it by reading books, attending seminars, and listening to webinars as well as networking with others who can help you in some way such as contractors of various specialties, other investors, real estate agents, loan officers, bankers, etc. If you need to learn, this book will give you a good start.

These three things are going to work together to help you build financial wealth. They are synergistic, and your efforts are multiplied as you spend time learning about the process and capturing the power of leverage and what it can do for you. Please realize you can start your journey no matter where you are in life if you will put in some time to learn the basics, build on what you know, and start investing now, no excuses.

Chapter 1 Summary

In order to achieve true financial wealth, you need to be an investor. You need to have an "investor" mindset, one that thinks in terms of possibilities. Don't think your current income and savings plan will be enough to build true wealth. Don't place limits on your financial potential. When I first started out, I didn't think I could do it either, but my first husband's dream became my dream. When we divorced and I found myself a single mother and a landlord, I picked up the ball and ran with it. I took control of my finances and my future. If I could do it, you can, too.

Chapter 2

Strategies for Investing

There are a few basics to consider when making your investment plan. Remember, in this book, I will share mine with you, but you must choose your own strategy. Looking back, when I first started, it was my ex-husband who picked the properties. They were certainly not ones I would even consider buying today. The important thing to remember, though, is that your first property does not have to be something you would ever consider living in; it does not have to be a status symbol. You start with what you can afford and choose criteria that make sense for you. You can pick other criteria, but you must look for cash flow and potential for appreciation, because without cash flow you are dead in the water. And you must take action. Reading this book, going to investment clubs and learning about real estate investing will not do you any good unless you set some realistic goals, put them in writing, and decide on your own personal strategy for investing. You and I are different, but I think you can learn from my experience. The one thing that keeps people poor is the fear of buying their first house. I am hoping to get you past that. It's not that complicated.

One of the things I find about most books on real estate investing, they are pretty basic, and they talk about different strategies, such as wholesaling; options; rehabbing; flipping; buy, rent, and hold; owner financing, and others; but they lack the personal experiences of someone who has done these things and knows how it worked out for them. I am going to tell you about my personal journey, in hopes that it will help you not make the same mistakes I did and that the things I think I did right will be a help to you as you take your journey.

Wholesaling - the sale of goods to anyone other than the standard consumer

Option contract - a contract on a specific piece of real estate that allows the buyer the exclusive right to purchase the property for a period of time

Rehabbing - buying a house that needs to be rehabilitated, getting the work done, and then selling it for a profit

Flipping – buying a house and reselling it for a higher price in a short period of time

Let's talk about how to pick a property. Criteria are the things you should consider when a buying opportunity presents itself. Today, when I am picking criteria, I look for the greatest opportunity with the least amount of risk. Criteria that matter to me today in 2016 are location, age, 3 bedrooms, 2 bathrooms, decent schools. I prefer no septic tank, single family homes priced below the average of homes in the surrounding area and located in an area that is trending upward. Most of this data can be found on sites like Zillow®, which is free, and there are also many other places online you can go to research neighborhoods. Below is an example of a home I purchased for $86,000 in 2014, the current Zestimate® is now $127,245 and the rent estimate is $1150. (See below example of a current house I own located at 4220 Crosswinds Dr, Milton, FL 32583. Additional details are available on Zillow®.)

4220 Crosswinds Dr,
Milton, FL 32583

$86,000

Sold

4
Beds

2
Baths

1,515
Sq Ft

Edit Facts Add Photos Share

Your Zestimate

Add owner estimate

Zestimate ❓	Rent Zestimate ❓
$127,245	**$1,150/mo**
+$1,210 Last 30 days	+$0 Last 30 days

My first husband picked the properties we bought. I honestly don't think he gave this factor any thought because every one of those first investment properties were in bad neighborhoods, and I have since learned to look at crime data and stay away from properties in high crime areas. I do have some lifelong memories and stories to share about lessons learned and being a landlord. I will never forget that day back years ago when as I was flipping through the TV channels, I recognized a familiar face of one of my tenants on a local cop show that featured locals being arrested for various crimes. She was being arrested for shooting at her husband while having a domestic dispute. I cannot adequately describe my dismay, but the thought of shooting my ex-husband for buying that house may have crossed my mind for a brief second! Luckily, she was a bad shot and her husband was barely injured because he got the hell out of the house just in time shutting the door behind him so it was kind of a blind shot. The new steel exterior door we had installed not long before the incident had a bullet hole in it none the less, and it served to remind me of that incident for many years. It also brings to light the importance of the old real estate adage I learned to use as one of my criteria for future purchases: simply put, "location, location, location."

Today, you can use the Internet to check out the neighborhood, the crime data, schools, etc. and as a real estate agent I can go into the local MLS and set criteria I want and those I absolutely do not want. By the way, the Internet was not around when I started buying and selling real estate, but I surely do use it now every day and so do more than 91% of the real estate buyers and sellers today, so you should use it too. That does not substitute for a drive by though. If you are the investor and you are in doubt about a neighborhood of a home you are considering purchasing, you need to personally drive by the home more than 1 time to check out the neighborhood. I have found that by far the best time to check it out is after dark in your car, especially on the weekends. Keep windows up and doors locked on your journey. If you have a real estate agent, you should not ask the agent or the listing agent of the property to do this for you as you would be asking them to violate Federal Housing Laws that have been put in place to protect the public against discrimination. Sites I frequently use to check neighborhoods are http:// neighborhoodscout.com and http://city-data.com. You should also research and learn about the neighborhood's past and try to get a picture of where it is going. Consider researching the overall appreciation rate in the neighborhood compared to other neighborhoods you are considering. You may not be aware, but that information is available on sites like Zillow® and RealtyTrac®. Note in the example above, the property on Crosswinds had appreciated $1210 in the 30 days prior to this report. If the values are the same or going downward, you may not want this property as a long-term investment. Check more than one site, as this data is not always 100%, especially if there are not a lot of recent sales, or if there are not very many rentals in a given area it may be difficult to rely on the rent Zestimate® in Zillow®. In the case of the Crosswinds property example above, I feel both the sales and rent Zestimates® are fairly accurate at this time.

There are many other types of criteria you can set. Ask yourself: do you want to buy single- family residences; multifamily, which can be duplexes, quadraplexes, or apartment buildings; office buildings; or freestanding commercial properties?

Let's review the types of ownership structure and the types of properties themselves you may choose to invest in, as well as the different ways you can structure rental agreements for specialty properties.

→ **Condominium (Condo for short)** - A residential building with multiple units in which each unit inside the building is individually owned. Each owner has exclusive right to his or her unit and has a "common interest" in the common areas.

→ **Cooperative ownership (co-op)** - You own shares in the corporation or a partnership or trust, but you do not specifically own your own apartment unit. Basically, it is the same as being a stockholder. Co-ops generally limit how you can rent your property and may not produce the highest financial returns.

→ **Duplex/triplex/Quadplex** - a residential property owned by one individual that may contain two/three/four units. Each unit has its own outside entrance.

→ **Townhouse** - This is like a hybrid of a single-family home and a condo. These are individually-owned residential properties that are connected by a common wall, and the owner owns both the structure and the land beneath the structure, as well as part of the common areas.

→ **Single-Family Residential -** A self-standing residential property under single ownership, designed to be lived in by one family.

→ **Multifamily Residential -** properties designed to accommodate many families, such as apartment complexes. Apartment complexes may or may not have separate outside entrances, and they usually have no separate yard space, just common areas for parking and recreational use.

→ **Time-Share/Partial Ownership -** You own the right to use the property for a fixed amount of time.

→ **Commercial Property -** This could be anything from hotels, apartment complexes, warehouses, office space, retail, industrial or manufacturing centers, and more.

Any of these types can be used as investment property and purchased for long- or short-term investment.

There are different ways you can rent property. You can rent unfurnished or furnished, long or short term. In order to decide on a good strategy for you, you should consider your long-term investment goals for the property. Is your goal to build equity, create a positive monthly cash flow? Or is it to rent it out for a time, then sell later at a profit? You should also keep in mind things like how much time you have to take care of and manage your property.

Single family homes come with monthly expenses like trash removal, power and water bills, and yard maintenance. If you own a condo, you pay a monthly assessment, regardless of whether someone is living in the unit. You should check and see what costs are included in the monthly maintenance fee, most include exterior maintenance, trash and the insurance for the building, but many do not include water inside the units. Keep in mind, you must pay the assessments monthly regardless of if someone is living in the unit.

I, personally, like to rent my homes unfurnished and long term. I get a signed 12-month lease and make the tenants responsible for all the utilities, yard maintenance, pest control, and some minor maintenance. Consistency and continuity are two benefits of investing in this type of rentals, and it takes the least amount of time and effort. Tenants often stay and renew their lease beyond the first year. I find the average length of time in our area tenants stay in the same place is about three years. In Pensacola, Florida, for instance, we have a large number of military renters and they come in two types. Students attending the flight training program or another school tend to stay one year or less. Military families typically get their orders for three to four years in one location, and if they like the home they are living in they will stay the entire time.

Student housing is another rental niche that is very viable in areas located near a college or university. If you are considering investing in student housing, take the time to visit the housing offices on local college or university campuses and ask what's currently available and what students are looking for in terms of housing. Undergraduates typically share housing, so be prepared for the unexpected, but you can charge more, and, therefore, it can produce a higher return. Again these students typically will find a place and renew their lease if they are happy with the landlord and the accommodations, so there is the potential for a four-year rental. Sometimes, students even replace themselves when they leave and refer new renters to take over.

Another kind of rental you can own is a corporate monthly rental. This is usually a lease for a minimum of 30 days on a month-to-month lease. The rental is completely furnished with housewares, a fully-equipped kitchen and electronics. Utilities are included in the monthly rate. The monthly rent is typically considerably higher than it is for annual rentals, and it can be a great option for people who want to use the home themselves for a portion of the year; however, it comes with greater risk of vacancy as well as theft of or damage to items left in the home .

The last option for residential property is vacation rentals. Vacation rentals are residential properties located in resort areas that are leased for less than 30 days to vacationing individuals and families. Vacation rentals are priced by the day or week and often will have repeat clients. Again, these rentals must be fully furnished and also include everything a family needs while they vacation such as dishes, pots and pans, towels, sheets, TV, wireless Internet and cable TV! Many of these rentals are also seasonal, unless you are located someplace like Hawaii where there is a consistent demand for vacation rentals all year around. Many people get interested in the idea of vacation rentals because they want to spend time vacationing in them as well, and they can be very lucrative, but it can require a lot of your own personal time to find regular weekly tenants. You can use a management company, but the cost of short term management is a lot higher than the cost of professional management for long term unfurnished rentals. My research has shown that in some locales, they charge up to 30% of the monthly rent for management. The rent includes all utilities, so you are paying on the gross rent, and then you still have to pay out the money for these things. I did an investment analysis and what I came up with showed that you would have to have it rented more than 50% of the year just to cover the mortgage, management, condo fees, utilities and other expenses. In Pensacola our season is between Memorial Day Weekend and Labor Day weekend which is over three months where it will likely be rented most if not all the weeks, but the rest of the time, there is no guarantee of regular bookings as many units sit empty much of the rest of the year, and you are not guaranteed bookings. If you are considering a vacation rental, please know that this is a higher level of risk, and make sure you are aware of all the costs involved. I like to say if you can afford it as a second home and just want to get additional income to help cover the costs, then it is a great way to go, and be prepared to be hands on to help get bookings for your unit.

Keep in mind that there are different types of vacation rentals, from the mountains to golf resorts to freshwater lakes or beaches. Generally, beach properties pose an even higher risk because of hurricanes, and if there was a hurricane such as the one we had 12 years ago, you still have to pay the mortgage and the condo fees even during post-hurricane renovations, and it most likely would not be able to be rented while those were being completed. After hurricane Ivan in 2004, some condos on Pensacola Beach lost one to two years of rental bookings because the project was undergoing reconstruction.

Commercial properties are also a viable income producing investment, but there are so many different types of commercial properties that would be the topic of another entire book, so I am not going to spend a lot of time on this subject. I do believe commercial properties are good investments for individuals who are running a small business and want to own rather than rent space in which to operate their business, experienced investors with larger amounts of cash and resources, large pools of investors often known as Real Estate Investment Trusts (REITS) or companies with large amounts of money they must invest to get a good long term rate of return such as life insurance companies. They are not something I would recommend for a beginning investor unless you have a specific use for the space. For example, I already own the building that houses my real estate business, and my company also bought a commercial foreclosure last year for less than $200,000 which we used approximately half of the space to open a small satellite office on the other side of town and rented the other half the building to a shop.

When you have found a property or properties you think would be a great investment, it is time to do a thorough evaluation of your choice before making an offer. You definitely want to look at things like the price per square foot.

Price per square foot = asking price divided by the total square footage

Everything being equal, if you have 2 units in the same complex, they should fall into the same range, so go to public records or other sources like Zillow® and be sure to find out how much similar properties in the same complex or neighborhood have sold for within the past 6 months, and you will get an idea of how good your deal is by comparing price per square foot on both the rental and sales prices. If you are buying multi-unit buildings such as duplexes or quads or other apartments, you want to evaluate those in terms of price per unit, and if the units are all the same number of bedrooms and similar floorplans, they should rent for about the same amount. Rents are usually based on the number of bedrooms: one bedroom apartments rent for less than two bedrooms, and so on.

Price per unit = asking price divided by the number of units

You can also consider property condition, amenities and upgrades when setting rent prices, and these things can also affect the asking price of the property you are considering. One thing I have found is that homes with outdated kitchens and old appliances will rent for less than those with a modern kitchen and newer appliances. Ceiling fans, updated lighting, wood or wood laminate flooring, hot tubs and swimming pools can have a positive effect on rent prices and days on the market. Outdated features may cause lower rents and more vacancies. I bought a duplex a couple of years ago that had old cabinets in both kitchens and butcher block countertops. It was built in the early '80s and had never had anything done to the kitchens, but the countertops and brown stained cabinets were in okay shape in unit A, so I thought I would try and rent it without making any changes. Unit B looked rough, so I had the cabinets painted white and had new countertops and appliances put in, and it rented right away. Weeks went by and unit A was still for rent. I had the cabinets painted an espresso color and put new brushed nickel hinges and door pulls, and since the countertops were in good shape I had a handyman apply a resurfacing product in an off-white color, and the appliances were okay so I had some new marketing photos taken and the property rented right away. Another cheap fix is removing or painting over outdated wallpaper or paneling. This can transform the look of a bathroom in a flash. Seems like a little thing, but when you buy a property, don't cut too many corners or you will cut your profits in the long run; do it right, and you can rent it faster for more money!

How picky you want to be is going to depend upon your personal level of risk as well as things like cash flow and the cost of insurance. In Florida, where I live, I also usually as a rule try to stay away from properties that are already in a flood zone or may be in the future because the insurance rates are higher and you need a separate flood policy at an additional cost. It would be prudent for you to check with an insurance agent in the area you plan to buy investments in to see if there are any specialty riders you need to include in your policy pertinent to that area, and make sure you ask for a landlord's policy if you will be renting the home. If you plan to fix it and flip or only hold it short term and the home will be vacant, you must purchase vacant house insurance or if under renovation, a contractors or builders risk policy.

I try to avoid properties that have a pool because pools cost a lot to maintain and are an additional liability. You can set other criteria such as no septic tanks, only brick homes, three or more bedrooms, but don't get too carried away in the details as you may have no choices left to pick from. I found that I have to adjust my criteria as the market adjusts. When the economy is bad, there are more deals readily available. When the economy improves, I may be competing against others, dealing with multiple offers and need ready cash to even get considered as a buyer for a particular property. You can start with a broad category and work your way to the best properties that meet the most criteria.

The properties I bought in the early years in Pensacola ended up providing me with considerable cash flow over the years and still do today, but they definitely gave me a few gray hairs along the way. The reason they turned out so well is that they were all purchased with owner financing terms with about 10% down payment and an interest rate that was better than what the bank would give me in the 1980s.

The next criteria I feel is very important for any investor involves terms. These are things such as will you get a bank loan, pay cash, option, or ask the owner to finance. There is also the interest rate and the period of amortization, which is usually 15 or 30 years. Some banks are looking for a balloon in five years, which means they can call the loan due after five years or renegotiate the terms. Balloon mortgages are used a lot in commercial lending.

Interest Rate - A rate which is charged or paid for the use of money. An interest rate is often expressed as an annual percentage of the principal and is calculated by dividing the amount of interest by the amount of the principal. If the interest is $90 in a year on a loan of $1000, then the interest rate would be 90/1000 x100% = 9%.

APR - the effective rate on a loan after subtracting required loan fees from the face amount of the loan. Unless the loan involves no required closing costs, the APR will always be higher than the actual interest rate.

Amortization-When used in the context of a home purchase, amortization is the process by which loan principal decreases over the life of a loan. With each mortgage payment that is made, a portion of the payment is applied towards reducing the principal, and another portion of the payment is applied towards paying the interest on the loan. An **amortization schedule**, a table detailing each periodic payment on a loan, shows this ratio of principal and interest and demonstrates how a loan's principal amount decreases over time.

Balloon payment mortgage – A mortgage which does not fully amortize over the term of the note, thus leaving a balance due at maturity. The final payment is called a balloon payment because of its large size. An example of a balloon payment mortgage would be a loan that is amortized over 30 years with a balloon payment for the balance of the note due at the end of 60 months.

I will tell you that terms can make or break a deal. Terms are one of the biggest reasons real estate is such a good long term investment. You can negotiate terms in any market, so with the right terms, a deal that might not meet one of your criteria becomes a great deal. The first duplex I owned was purchased as an owner occupant with a VA loan which means we had 100% financing. But we had income. When you put no money down, any cash flow and future income gets you a 100% rate of return. The reason for this is called leverage. Webster's definition of leverage as it relates to real estate is as follows: the use of credit to enhance one's speculative capacity. There is no other investment that allows you to make little or no down payment, let someone else pay for it, and reap all the rewards. It really doesn't get better than that.

Financial Leverage – the cost of money borrowed compared to overall rate of return

Positive Leverage – rate of return is greater than the cost (interest rate) of the borrowed funds.

Example: $100,000 x .10 = $10,000 Net Operating Income

$ 80,000 x .05 = $ 4,000 Annual Interest Payments

$ 6,000 New Net Cash Flow

You only had to use $20,000 of your own money to purchase the investment and borrowed $80,000 at 5%, your new rate of return is $6,000 divided by $20,000 = 30%

Neutral Leverage – The cost of borrowing is the same as the rate of return. Neutral leverage does not affect the investment's rate of return, either positively or negatively.

Negative Leverage – The cost of borrowing money is greater than the rate of return.

Example: $100,000 x .10 = $10,000 Net Operating Income

$ 80,000 x .11 = $8,800 Annual Interest Payments

$1,200 divided by $20,000 = 6%

Negative leverage decreases the investment's rate of return. A thorough understanding of the types of leverage is the only way to determine how much money you can borrow without adversely affecting the investment's rate of return.

I am going to give you some examples of the power of financial leverage. Let's use a $100,000 home for this example. In today's market, unless you are buying a duplex and plan to live in one unit like I did, you will most likely have to get a bank or private loan to purchase the property and put down up to 20% or $20,000. Let's say you get a mortgage loan at 5% interest rate, and your payments including PITI (a mortgage payment that is the sum of monthly principal, interest, taxes, and insurance) are $650 a month. You can get $1000 a month rent for the property, which in today's market is doable (I currently have three properties that cost less than $100,000 each that were purchased in 2014 and 2015 that are all rented for between $1,000 and $1,100 a month). Let's also assume that rents go up 2% a year, and you plan to sell in 10 years. Assuming you hire professional management and with other reasonable expenses, your cash flow before taxes in the first year is $5160, which is a 23.45% cash on cash rate of return, and your equity buildup is $1180 from payments made on the principal. Assuming a 2% rent increase per year and a modest 2% property appreciation per year, a 28% personal income tax rate as well as listing with a professional realtor when you sell, the after tax proceeds of the sale could be over $40,000, and your cash flow during the 10 years would have been almost

$50,000! These are not pie in the sky; these are real numbers. Leverage is a powerful tool you can use to build wealth with real estate.

Cash-on-cash rate of return = cash flow per year divided by the amount of the initial investment. In the example above $5160 is the cash flow and $20,000 is the initial investment, so $5160 divided by $20,000=23.45%

Equity is the difference between the market value of an investment property and the balance owed on the mortgage loan.

Before we go on, there are a few other components that contribute to the overall rate of return of a particular real estate investment. These are important because real estate is one of the only investments that combines all four of these components.

The first is appreciation, which is an increase or rise in the value. Even modest appreciation over time will greatly influence the rate of your return. Next, there is loan amortization, which takes into consideration the portion of each payment that goes toward principal reduction. Third is the cash flow generated from the property, and fourth is the tax benefits that can come with owning real estate.

Immediate tax benefits come when you own rental real estate because you are allowed to deduct all your expenses except the amount of your mortgage payment that is applied toward reducing the principal loan balance, and you can also depreciate residential real estate over time.

Depreciation-an income tax deduction that allows a taxpayer to recover the cost or other basis of certain property. It is an annual allowance for the wear and tear, deterioration, or obsolescence of the property.

Appreciation- an increase or rise in the value of a property

Measuring a Real Estate Investment

With any measurement based on a future prediction or hypothetical, we know that many parameters, events, and more can change the results. But that shouldn't stop us from doing our due diligence on the front end of investment properties. Let's take a look at the kinds of properties I focus on.

Annual rental income: $1,000 per month rents less 2% vacancy = $980 x 12 = $11,760 per year. Basic view: invested $20,000 (down payment) for 10 years and cashed out with a hypothetical $66,267 = ~12.7% rate of return. Rate of return is an approximate just to show value. The below summary is from a calculator created by David L. Anderson and has been reprinted with his permission and uses only a modest 2% per year appreciation factor for the value of the real estate, as well as 2% annual increases in rents and expenses. It summarizes a 10 year holding period and an investor in the 28% tax bracket. The initial investment grew from $20,000 invested to cash out at the sale of $66,267, which is more than three times the amount invested!

The annual property data, shown in the first chart below, is used to estimate income and expenses and is something I learned over the years which helps make the initial determination about the feasibility of an investment. Things to take into account are estimated rents, how long it will take to rent the property, anticipated operating expenses, what the cash flow will be after paying the mortgage, and other expenses but before taking taxes into account. You can also use this type of analysis to check the rate of return for any existing properties you may have. This rate of return is before taxes, so you should consult your tax advisor for advice on the income tax implications of a particular investment.

Market Value:	$100,000
Purchase Price:	$100,000
Loan Amount:	$80,000
Loan Interest Rate:	5.00%
Loan Period (Years):	30
Illustration Period (Years):	10
Net Investment Growth Rate (COM):	4.00%
Tax Bracket:	28.00%
Capital Gains Tax Rate:	15.00%
Interest Only (Yes=1, No=0):	0

Down Payment:	$20,000
Principal & Interest Payment:	$429
Interest-Only Payment:	$333
Extra Cost of Mortgage Repayment:	$96
Future Value of Investing Extra Cost:	$14,154

Monthly Investment Needed to Repay Loan:	$115
Monthly Cash Flow:	$292
Annual Cash Flow:	$3,500

Growth Rate of Real Estate:	2.00%
Annual Rental Income:	$11,760
Annual Property Tax:	$1,452
Annual Property Insurance:	$1,200
Annual Management/Misc Fees:	$1,176
Amount to Depreciate:	$80,000
Capital Gains Tax Exclusion:	$0
Annual % Increase for Income & Expenses:	2.00%
Selling Costs in Percentage:	7.00%
Closing Costs:	$0
Amount of Deductible Closing Costs:	$0

Cost Basis Less Depreciation:	$70,909

FV of Property:	$121,899
Income Less Expense (No Depreciation):	$49,927
Principal Part of Loan Payment:	-$14,927
Compound Tax Savings:	-$6,468
Remaining Debt:	-$65,074
Capital Gains Tax:	-$3,285
Taxable Gain on Depreciation Deduction:	-$7,273
Selling Costs:	-$8,533
Total Cash Out After Sell:	$66,267

Annual Property Data

Property Address	Anywhere, USA			
Date	07/08/16			Annual
Purchase Price/Value			$	100,000
Acquisition Costs			$	2,000
	First Mortgage Loan-to-Value	80%	$	80,000
	Rate 5,000% Term	30 years		
	Payment	$429.46		
	Second Mortgage Loan-to-Value	0%	$	0
	Rate Term	30 years		
	Payment	$0		
Gross Scheduled Income	Monthly	$1,000	$	12,000
Less Vacancy Allowance		2%	$	240
Gross Operating Income			$	11,760
Less Operating Expenses				
	Property Taxes		$	1,210
	Insurance		$	1,000
	Utilities		$	0
	Repairs		$	500
	Maintenance		$	0
	Management		$	1,176
	HOA		$	0
	Advertising		$	0
	Other Expenses		$	0
	Total Operating Expenses		$	3,886
Net Operating Income			$	7,874
Less Annual Debt Service	Mortgage principle and interest payments		$	5153.49
Cash Flow Before Taxes			$	2,721
Cash on Cash				12.37%
Equity Build-up, Year 1		$1,180.29		5.36%

Brantley

The table below shows projections into the future for end of year one, five and ten. It shows the decrease in the loan amount and the increased build-up of equity using an estimate of a modest 3% appreciation. It also shows annual income increasing due to increase of rents an average of 2% a year and increase in expenses of 1%. These are the numbers I am using for illustration purposes only and are not guaranteed. Actual results could be better or not as good as the projections below.

Increase Projections

Property Anywhere, USA	Annual Appreciation	3.00%	
Date 07/08/16	Annual Income Increase	2.00%	
	Annual Expense Increase	1.00%	
End of Years	**1**	**5**	**10**
(All values in $ unless otherwise noted)			
Purchase Price/Value	103,000	115,927	134,392
First Mortgage	78,820	73,463	65,074
Second Mortgage	0	0	0
Equity Build-up, Cumulative	1,180	6,537	14,926
(Amortization)			
Gross Scheduled Income			

End of Years	1	5	10
Monthly Rent @ $1,000	12,000	13,249	14,628
Less Vacancy Allowance- 2%	240	265	293
Gross Operating Income	11,760	12,984	14,335
Less Operating Expenses			
Property Taxes	1210	1284	1,363
Insurance	1000	1062	1,127
Utilities	0	0	0
Repairs	500	531	563
Maintenance	0	0	0
Management	1,176	1,248	1,325
HOA	0	0	0
Advertising	0	0	0
Other Expenses	0	0	0
Total Operating Expenses	3,886	4,125	4,379
Net Operating Income	7,874	8,859	9,957
Less Annual Debt Service	5,153	5,153	5,153
Cash Flow Before Taxes	2,721	3,705	4,803
Equity Build-up	1,180	1,441	1,849
Cash on Cash	12.37%	16.84%	21.83%
Equity Build-up	5.36%	6.55%	8.41%

The three tables below show the future wealth position and where the numbers come from if you hold the property for a period of 10 years. They show what you can expect to gain upon the sale of the property as well as what your total rates of return are projected to be over the 10-year period. A 25% personal tax bracket and 15% capital gains tax are the numbers used for these projections. These are projections only. Please consult your tax advisor for accurate info pertaining to your current tax situation.

Investment Analysis Summary

Property Address	Anywhere, USA		
Initial Investment	(Down Payment + Acquisition Costs)	$	22,000
Annual Cash Flow	Before Taxes, Year 1	$	2,721
Annual Cash Flow	After Taxes, Year 1	$	2,913
Property Address	**Anywhere, USA**		
Holding Period in Years			10
After Tax Proceeds from Sale		$	50,333
Future Wealth Position	After Tax Proceeds+ Accumulated Cash Flows	$	99,745
Cash on Cash, Year 1	Cash Flow Before Tax/Initial Investment		12.37%
Equity Build-up, Year 1	Amortization Year 1/ Initial Investment		5.36
Before-tax Rate of Return			19.27%
After-tax Rate of Return			13.87%
	Wealth Position Contribution Appreciation		43%
	Amortization (Equity Build-up)		19%
	Cash Flows		38%

Contributing Factors	Cap Rate	Cash on Cash	Rate of Return
Cash Flows	x	x	X
Leverage		x	X
Equity Build-up			X
Appreciation			X
Tax Savings			X

Investment Analysis-Detail 1

Property Address	Anywhere, USA			
First Year Income Analysis				
Gross Scheduled Income			$	12,000
Less Vacancy Allowance			$	240
Gross Operating Income			$	11,760
Less Total Operating Expenses			$	3,886
Net Operating Income			$	7,874
Less Annual Debt Service on 1ST mortgage		$429.46	$	5,153
Less Annual Debt Service on 2ND mortgage		$0	$	0
Cash Flow Before Taxes			$	2,721
Net Operating Income			$	7,874
Less First Year's Interest		$3,866.67	$	3,867
Less Cost Recovery			$	2,909
Tax Liability (Savings)			$	308
Cash Flow Before Taxes-Year 1			$	2,721
Cash Flow After Taxes-Year 1			$	2,413

Investment Analysis-Detail 2

Property Address	Anywhere, USA		
Value at Time of Purchase		$	100,000
Projected Sales Price		$	134,392
Less Projected Cost of Sale		$	8,063
Less Adjusted Basis		$	72,909
Total Taxable Gain on Sale		$	53,419
Total Cost Recovery Taken		$	29,091
Recapture Tax Rate			25%
Tax Due from Recapture		$	7,273
Balance of Capital Gain		$	24,328
Capital Gain Tax Rate			15%
Tax Due on Balance at Capital Gains Rate		$	3,649
Total Tax Due			10,922
Projected Sales Price		$	134,392
Less Projected Cost of Sale		$	8,063
Less 1st Mortgage Balance		$	65,074
Less 2nd Mortgage Balance		$	0
Less Total Tax Due		$	10,922
After-tax Proceeds from Sale		$	50,333
Holding Period (years)			10
Cash Flows Accumulated End of Holding Period		$	30,308
Total Future Wealth		$	80,640
Initial Investment		$	22,000
Before-tax Rate of Return			19.27%
After-tax Rate of Return			13.87%

Investment Analysis Assumptions

The following is a list of assumptions used to make the investment analysis that accompanies this presentation:

→ There is a constant appreciation rate during the holding period.

→ Rental Income and expenses will change according to variable that is set.

→ Investor wants to maximize wealth and will reinvest positive cash flows.

→ If negative cash flows result, an interest charge will be made at the same savings rate to offset the opportunity cost of being able to use that money elsewhere.

→ The marginal tax rate of the investor will remain constant during the holding period.

→ The marginal tax rate of the investor is used to determine the impact of this investment, regardless of what else the investor may do in the year of sale.

→ The investor is able to apply the annual tax savings generated against that year's tax liability.

→ The investor will pay federal taxes for long term capital gains and recapture of cost recovery in the year of the sale.

→ Before-tax and after-tax rates of return are determined for holding period with adjustments made for income and expenses.

→ The cash flow accumulation takes into consideration the adjustments made for income and expense increases.

→ no consideration is made regarding a possible additional 3.8% LTCG (long term capital gains) tax applying to certain investors in upper income brackets. If an investor is concerned that there may be an additional tax liability due to their individual circumstances, they should contact their tax professional and make adjustments accordingly.

Allocations prior to expenses paid are used to approximate contribution percentages.

In the illustrations above, I used a 3% per year property appreciation and 2% increase in rents to come up with the projections over time. Of course, sometimes properties appreciate more or less, but you can see that over time because of the combination of leverage and compounding as well as the modest appreciation and pay down of the principal balance of the loan which of course you should thank your tenant for regularly, the rates of return go from 12.37% in year one to 21.83% in year 10. By using borrowed funds when you believe the income from the asset and asset price appreciation will be more than the cost of borrowing, you are taking advantage of the tremendous power of leverage and how you can use that to help you with your goal of building wealth. Please note, I used 10 years as the holding period. This is to illustrate the power of real estate as a long-term, not a short-term investment.

Once you start getting cash flow from your properties, you should start to have capital of your own to reinvest. In the case of the rental home I just illustrated to you, the cash flow from the rents alone saved and reinvested would be enough to purchase at least two to three more properties over the ten-year period of time. The cash flow from the additional properties would allow you to purchase more, and all the while your tenants are paying them off for you.

Don't forget I have included property management services in the projections. A property manager helps you with the headaches such as finding and choosing your tenants, screening, handling the day-to-day maintenance calls, and late rents. The money just comes to your bank account monthly; this is the passive income we speak of that builds wealth over time. If you prefer to do the management yourself, you would have even better cash flow; however, management is not as easy as it looks, so beware of stepping into management, unless you study the issues and are aware of the state and federal laws that you need to obey.

Another thing real estate does is to protect against inflation. In economics, inflation is a sustained increase in the general price level of goods and services in an economy over a period of time. When the price level rises, each unit of currency buys fewer goods and services. Consequently, inflation reflects a reduction in the purchasing power per unit of money. In times of inflation, house prices will rise, along with rents and interest rates, usually. If you own a house which is leveraged with a low interest, fixed-rate mortgage, like we have available in 2016, you will benefit from leverage, and your house payment will stay about the same (except for possible rises in taxes and insurance);

you will collect more rent from your tenants and benefit from more rapid appreciation of your asset. Our current historically-low interest rates make this an even better time to invest and take out a mortgage.

We talk a lot about the term millionaire. What does it really mean to be a millionaire? How many millionaires do we really have in America, the land of plenty?

According to Wikipedia®, millionaire households constitute roughly seven percent of all American households, and half of those are headed by retirees. There are multiple approaches to determining a person's status as a millionaire. One of the two most commonly used measurements is net worth, which counts the total value of all property owned by a household minus the household's debts. According to this definition, a household owning an $800k home, $50k of furnishings, two cars worth $60k, a $60k retirement savings account, $45k in mutual funds, and a $325k vacation home with a $250k mortgage, $40k in car loans, and $25k in credit card debt would be worth about $1,025,000; and every individual in this household would thus be a millionaire. However, according to the measurement used for some specific applications, such as evaluating an investor's expected tolerance for risk for stockbroker ethics, equity in one's principal residence is excluded, as are lifestyle assets, such as the car and furniture. Therefore, the above example household would only have net financial assets of $105,000. Another term used is net investable assets or working capital.

When people first start investing in real estate or even just thinking about it, they are concerned about risk and also about the fact that it often seems to take a lot of time for the investment to "payoff." The short-term benefits just don't seem to balance out the short-term sacrifices of time, money, and effort.

I have a simple illustration about how money works that illustrates the power of compounding and the power of negotiating favorable terms. When I first heard this story and saw figures similar to those on the chart below, I had to recalculate the numbers myself to truly believe it could be true. This story has nothing to do with real estate investing; it has to do with how money works. Terms apply to money in general, the money you earn and how you spend it. This story is about a worker who was offered a reasonable wage for one month's work. Instead of agreeing to the normal pay, he negotiated a scale where his pay started with just one penny the first day and doubled every day that followed. The employer shook on the deal thinking she was getting a great deal but, unfortunately for her, results in an invoice at the end of the month totaled 10.7 million dollars. I am grateful that one was never pulled on me !

Daily Doubling

Days	Daily Wage ($)
1	0.01
2	0.02
4	0.08
5	0.16
6	0.32
7	0.64
8	1.28
9	2.56
10	5.12
11	10.24
Days	**Daily Wage ($)**
12	20.48
13	40.96
14	81.92
15	163.84
16	327.68
17	655.36
18	1,310.72
19	2,621.44

20	5,242.88
21	10,485.76
23	41,943.04
24	83,886.08
25	167,772.16
26	335,544.32
27	671,088.64
28	1,342,177.28
29	2,684,354.56
30	5,368,709.12
31	10,737,418.24

No matter how little money or knowledge you have now, the trick is to get started and let the power of compounding and growth of your investments take you to reach your personal level of financial wealth and a secure future.

Chapter 2 Summary

The two important things to consider when evaluating an investment are criteria and terms.

Examples of criteria are features of the property, neighborhoods, etc.

Examples of terms are cash, option contracts, owner financing, bank loans, loan-to-value ratios (mortgage value to appraised value), and rates of return.

Leveraging, compounding, and protecting against inflation are three big things that make long term investing in real estate so good for building wealth.

Chapter 3
Basics of Financial
Wealth Building

I, personally, like to use the term "wealth building" instead of "investing." Many people invest, but I want you to not only invest but also to use the gains you make from your investments to increase your net worth and build wealth. The concept of building financial wealth is not something you or I ever learned in high school or college. Somehow, it seems this is a concept that has fallen through the cracks of the educational system and left for people to figure out and learn on their own. I have found that most people today have not taken their financial education seriously. I am not going to be able to tell you everything you need to know in this book, but my goal is to give you enough information to allow you to further your education and take action. You have to get educated, read more books, listen to audio tapes, and attend seminars. Be careful when attending "free" seminars, a lot of seminars, especially the free or low cost ones, are merely an introductory infomercial that will try to motivate you to buy their books and tapes and expensive boot camps. I have been to those seminars with my latest husband, trying to get him to get educated, and although they have some merit, his motivation turned out to be temporary. We have since parted ways, partly because our financial goals and our values were not in sync. My advice to you is that you may need to separate your business dealings from your personal relationships, as those around you may or may not have the same goals as you do. When your spouse wants to spend and you want to save and invest, it can be difficult to keep on track with your goals.

Below are four definitions you need to know that relate to money and wealth. Let's call them the four Cs because they all start with the letter C.

→ Capital - money invested in something expected to grow in value

→ Cash flow - money generated from investments

→ Cash - money held in reserve

→ Consumption - money spent on anything not expected to grow in value

Investors build their financial lives on capital, while consumers (the majority of the population) build theirs on consumption. Investors see money as an opportunity to invest while consumers see money as an opportunity to spend. Consumers who earn a lot of money can give the appearance of wealth without any of the substance. Living life as an investor means you should first live a life where you consume less than you earn. Ask yourself, does your income go right out the door in the form of consumption or are you currently saving and investing? If you are a consumer, your first goal needs to be to change your mindset to that of an investor. Your long-term goal might be to own ten houses that are rented for cash flow, but how are you going to get there? You get there by educating yourself on how money works, saving some money by creating and sticking to a budget where you spend less than you earn, then learning how to find the best investments in your market that will generate cash flow. This does not happen overnight. If you have a lot of consumer (credit card) debt, a short-term goal might be to pay extra on that debt and pay it down so you can qualify for a mortgage instead. You may need to drive your car a while longer instead of trading it in on a new one.

Living life as an investor means you should first live a life where you consume less than you earn.

I like to say there are two kinds of debt: good and bad. Credit cards, car payments, and installment loans that carry high interest rates are "bad debt." Mortgages secured by real estate that are either your personal residence or rental property are "good debt." A good way to evaluate your debt is to look at the balances and interest rates and pay off the highest interest rate loans first by paying more than the minimum payment every month.

If you do not own a home yourself, the first investment I would recommend is to invest in your own home. Owner occupied loan rates are less, down payments can be little or nothing, and there are first time homebuyer programs that can help you get in and even pay most of your closing costs. When you buy that first home, think of it as an investment, try to get some equity on the buy by negotiating the best price and terms, and keep in mind that you are an investor, not a consumer, so remember to live slightly below your means so you can still set some money aside for investing. For most young investors, that first home might not be your dream home, but it is a start on the road to financial wealth.

You now need to start keeping track of something called your net worth, which is basically all your income and assets less your debts (liabilities). Don't worry if you do not own a home and you just graduated from college with student loans and credit card debt. Right now, your net worth may be a negative number, but you can turn it around quickly if you set realistic, specific, and measurable goals and take action today. You don't have to know anything about investing in real estate to change your attitude from that of a consumer to that of an investor. You can do that while reading this book, and that is the first step toward becoming a successful investor.

Let's talk about your primary residence as an investment. Remember, part of the beauty of real estate is that it can be leveraged, so you control an asset, but the bank is helping you pay for it monthly. Real estate in most markets is an appreciating asset, so as the value goes up, and you make the monthly payments, the loan balance goes down, creating equity, which will increase your net worth. You can refinance and use the equity in your home to pay off consumer debt or put up the down payment for another piece of real estate. You can turn your first home into a rental and buy something else for yourself, or you can sell it after two years of living there with no taxable gain on the sale. There are many ways to get started, which will all be discussed in the coming pages.

I am also going to tell you that life has a way of happening, and unless you keep on growing, you won't reach your goals. In my case, it was my second husband who had custody of his son and an unexpected baby. My son David was born when my oldest daughter was almost ten, and for a few years there, it was work: diapers, carpools, homework, and before I knew it, I had teenagers! I still had the cash flow from the properties which helped with the bills, but at one point, my husband quit his job to stay at home with the kids because my income as a nurse plus my investments were more than he could earn and the cost of day care and after school care was about the same as him staying home with the kids. There was no money left over for new investments, but I was glad for the cash flow from those rentals. I missed the real estate business, and I knew that I wanted to get back in it full-time; I just was not sure how, until I was at home recovering from cervical spine surgery and I got offered a job doing property management.

I never went back to my nursing job after that surgery; instead I ended up buying the business I went to work for after about a year on the job. At that time, there were about 120 management contracts and guaranteed income from those contracts even after I paid the seller of the business half the monthly income which was the terms I had agreed to for the purchase. It was not easy, but I knew that I could make it work, and my second husband was a great maintenance man, so he was able to get paid to do service work like appliance repair, painting, etc. I was then able to structure the deal so I could keep more of the income by paying off the seller with a loan from the bank. The seller agreed to a cash payoff about $10,000 less than what we originally had agreed to when I was paying them on terms, and I ended up with about $2000 a month more income just from restructuring that deal. This is an example of how good terms can make the deal better.

It was not long before opportunities to buy and rehab houses came my way and I was happy to be back in the real estate business full time. My second husband was a great help with the management business: his knowledge of maintenance and construction went hand in hand with my real estate knowledge, and for a while, things were good. Until in the year 2000, he was involved in a car accident and ended up with cervical spine and shoulder surgeries. After that, he was not able to do the work he had previously done for the business, so it was up to me to keep up the business and the income with not a lot of help from him. It was about that time I really started to want more from life, and I started reading books on success. In retrospect, I think it was an infomercial about Tony Robbins' audio series and workbook called *Personal Power* that started to change things for me back in about 2002. I was still investing in homes when the opportunity presented itself, and I was running my company, which was continuing to grow. I was living in Gulf Breeze which was about a 25-30 minute commute to Pensacola, and I listened to that series of tapes daily on my way to and from work. Tony was very inspirational. One of the first things Tony said was that I should demand more from myself than other people expect. I thought about that a lot, so I went on to learn what he calls his Ultimate Success Formula, which is basically the following:

Get clear on what you want. Take action (sometimes you have to break through your fears). Evaluate the results and see what's working and what's not working. If you don't get it right the first time, adjust your approach and try again.

I realized there was nothing here I did not already know —Tony just had a really good delivery. He inspired me to push outside my comfort zone and continue to learn and grow. I attended as many classes and investment seminars as I could. I bought and read books about investing and continued to invest, while I reinforced that knowledge by advising others on purchasing investment properties and helping them build a portfolio of rentals. One side benefit was that it increased the number of properties my company was managing. I was becoming an expert, and people were listening to my advice. I owned multiple rentals and made money doing flips and helping others.

Then came the housing bubble and by 2005 it was nearly impossible to find a deal that cash flowed except in very bad neighborhoods. I had to stop buying rentals. It was getting too crazy out there; I saw 30% appreciation happen almost overnight in our area. I knew I had never seen anything like that in Pensacola before. Some people were flipping condos for big money. I almost bought a presale condo but something told me not to. I decided to take a break from buying. I held on to most of what I had purchased as it was making a good cash flow. During this time I focused on listing and selling homes for my clients who wanted to make some quick cash in the inflated market here in Florida. Of course, I was always looking for deals, but they were hard to come by, so I decided to get some more education that helped me get to the next level.

At that time, my real estate office was located next to one of the financial planning firms in the area. I was making some great money listing and selling houses and the property management business had grown. Since I could not find many good deals, I was trying to find another investment vehicle that could get me a steady return until I could find more of the real estate deals I was looking for. Now, I will say there are deals in every market, but when there is a buying frenzy and inventory is low, deals are harder to get. Rents were up, but sales prices were so inflated that no matter how I worked the numbers I just could not get a good cash flow unless I went outside my criteria and went into neighborhoods that, in my opinion, were not desirable because of high crime and poor schools. I bought a house I thought would be a good investment in Gulf Breeze. The house had flooded in the hurricane, and it took longer than anticipated to get the rehab done, and during that time, I saw the market start to get soft. I thought I had a buyer, but that fell through, and after the house stayed empty about six months and prices were sliding in the wrong direction, I rented the home hoping that things would get better and I could sell it. Well, that never happened, at least not soon enough for me. This particular home became a long-term investment (always have a plan B), and it cash flowed well as a rental, but when I divorced in Dec 2011, the divorce settlement required me to liquidate this and other property so I could pay off my ex-husband his equity. The economy started to improve, and I finally did sell the house in 2013. It was not the best investment I ever made, but I did get most of my money back, and I had been renting it with very little vacancy for eight years. In reality, even though my net sale proceeds were about $22,000 less than what I had actually spent to purchase and rehab the home, I had collected over $90,000 in rent over the time I owned the home, so even my least profitable investment actually did make a net profit of over 3% a year according to my calculations.

I would like to go back to the time from late 2004 and 2005 when the real estate prices went up, and I had a conversation with one of the financial reps in the office next to me, and he explained their system which involved a series of financial educational sessions going over my current income, assets, debt, and cash flow, and I agreed to go through their program. I had to commit to several sessions, and it was there that I really got a better understanding of financial wealth and how to make money work for me aside from real estate. I learned the concept of arbitrage, which is what banks do. In short, banks take your money in your checking and savings accounts, and pay you a small amount of interest on your savings, and then they lend it to someone else at a higher rate of interest and make money off using your money: the difference is pure profit to the bank.

Since I already owned several pieces of real estate and some were mortgaged, I was at the point where I could no longer easily get a loan from the bank. The banks said my debt ratio was too high, even though I was making money off each one of my properties because they were all rented.

It was then my financial advisors taught me how I could actually become my own bank through the use of some special whole life insurance. They also taught me about the other benefits of whole life insurance, something I had grown up believing was bad and not for me at the time. After several sessions with the planner and reading a book called *Missed Fortune 101: A Starter Kit to Becoming a Millionaire* by Douglas R. Andrew, I bought an investment-grade, dividend-paying whole life insurance policy; and the planners taught me how to use it to my advantage and to become my own bank. At first, I thought it was too good to be true, but the more I read and learned, I realized it is actually like having your cake and eating it, too! I was taught how to increase the cash value faster, which, in reality, was a savings account inside the policy and the money was growing tax deferred. Did I tell you I could borrow against the policy? Every policy has a loan provision. There is no qualification; you just fill out a form, and they will give you an interest-only loan at a guaranteed interest rate without any of the closing costs typically charged by a mortgage company or hard money lender or cash advance fees charged by the credit card companies. I spent two years putting extra money into the policy, and when the market crashed in 2008, I had my own "bank" I could borrow money from to do the really great deals that came my way in the years after that. These planners also showed me how by paying extra money into the policy it would position me so that it could be paid up in five to seven years and it could grow and provide me tax-free retirement dollars later in life.

By then, I was also contributing to a Roth IRA, but there was a $5,000 a year maximum. Soon after that, my income became too much to allow me to put more into that Roth. However, the life insurance policy is really a lot like a Roth IRA, only better as it can passed on to your heirs tax-free. In these policies, although they have an initial face value, dividends from the company can be reinvested. Ultimately, these investments can potentially end up being worth more than the initial policy, and the cash value at the time of the policyholder's death can be transferred to the beneficiary tax-free.

Today, using my life insurance policy and my self-directed IRA, essentially I have my own "bank" which I can borrow money from at a fixed rate with no closing costs, use the money to purchase properties wholesale, rehab and flip houses. Enough said about life insurance. Depending on your situation, it may be something you want to consider. It has been valuable to me.

Arbitrage - buying in one market and simultaneously selling in another, profiting from a temporary difference. This is considered riskless profit. This is what banks do with the money we have on deposit.

Dividend - a distribution of a portion of a company's earnings, decided by the board of directors, to a class of its shareholders

Chapter 3 Summary

Get clear on what you want by setting realistic, specific goals.

Take action, first by getting educated and by finding others who have done what you want to do, learning from them, reading books, and attending meetings where other investors will be.

Evaluate your results.

Adjust your approach and try again.

Chapter 4

Different Strategies for Investing in Real Estate

There is no best strategy; they all have merit. I recommend you combine a quick cash strategy like wholesaling and/ or rehabbing and flipping with buy-and-hold, which will create long-term passive income from residential or commercial rentals. What is good about this strategy is the cash flow generated from the flips and wholesale deals can be used for down payments to purchase buy-and-hold properties.

First, let's talk about wholesaling. Wikipedia describes wholesaling as the sale of goods to anyone other than a standard consumer. As it relates to real estate, it is a short-term investment strategy to create profit by finding properties that can be purchased significantly below market value, and then either assigning the contract for a sum of money or closing the deal and reselling the property at a higher price. An example would go like this: you find a deal, and it may be in need of repairs that you do not want to make, so you then sell it to a rehabber who is willing to make the needed repairs. In this situation, you buy the property for one price and sell or "flip" it at a higher price. The difference would be profit. There are two methods that are commonly used; the first is 'assigning the contract." This is where you find another buyer before the closing who is willing to pay you to basically take over your existing contract using his or her own funds, and they step into your shoes as the buyer. The second way to wholesale is to have a double closing. This occurs when you close on the first property yourself then turn around and sell the property to a new buyer, usually on the same day or a short time later. This method may require you to obtain some funding source, either private money or a transactional lender to put up the money for you. These types of lenders are going to look more to the property than your credit score to determine if they will lend the money, and they will likely charge a higher interest rate than a conventional long-term mortgage, so make sure there is enough profit in the deal to minimize your risk.

Most real estate investors who wholesale also invest in other ways, but wholesaling is very popular because it is the quickest way to earn a profit on an investment. It is a good thing to learn as a beginning investor because with a relatively small deposit you can control a property worth significantly more, and you can learn to create a contract that has certain contingencies that allow you to back out. A contract would typically have an inspection contingency, which gives you a certain number of days to have the home inspected and if not satisfied with the inspection you can walk away and receive a refund of the deposit. You can also add a financing contingency, which means if you cannot get financing you can get released from the contract.

Since I am a real estate broker, I typically do things a little differently. Rather than agree to buy the property and wholesale it, if I feel it is a good property I get the seller to "list" it with me for sale, and I make my 6% commission and find an end buyer through my real estate brokerage. I do advertise and use some of the investor marketing techniques to help me find properties, and I have used wholesaling in the past, but those I do buy wholesale I typically rehab and sell to an end buyer. If you are a new investor, however, and do not have a real estate license or work full time in real estate, wholesaling can be a good avenue for you to get your feet wet in the world of real estate investing without needing a lot of money to start.

In order to be successful at wholesaling, you need three things: the first is "ability." Ability is increased with knowledge gained through reading, seminars, and mentors. Next, you need to spend time wisely. Two areas of focus for your time that can reap big benefits are networking and looking for properties that present an opportunity.

Let's talk a little about networking. Most successful real estate investors are also expert networkers and marketers. BNI®, Business Networking and Referrals, has had great success helping people learn to network and grow their businesses. They are the world's largest networking group with branches all over the world. If you want to invest in real estate, network with a local group such as BNI® and go to events where you can meet like-minded people. Look for a local REA (Real Estate Investors

Association). There are also online communities on social media sites such as Facebook and LinkedIn. You will want to network with people who can help you with your investment business, such as real estate agents, title agents, home inspectors, as well as divorce lawyers, estate planners and attorneys, real estate lawyers, and local lenders. You want to let everyone, including family, friends and other business associates, know about your investment business—anyone you can think of that might help you find motivated sellers or help you in your business. You will also most likely eventually want to get your own website and possibly have a blog about investing.

How do you find properties to wholesale? There are opportunities in every market. Think about personal forces such as relocation, marriage and divorce, birth of a child, bankruptcy, illness, job loss, and death as factors that could trigger a need to sell or buy real estate. There are also economic factors that will influence the real estate market. These are things such as job growth, interest rates, population shifts, and area revitalization. Neighborhoods change over time. Learn and keep your eye on the trends that are going on in your community. When you are networking, you not only need to look for potential sellers but you also need to build a buyers list that includes realtors, contractors, rehabbers, and other investors. When you find a property, you want to have a pool of buyers to offer it to. No one ever said it was easy; it takes a lot of time and effort, but I promise it will be worth the effort when you look back.

So let's jump in and talk about what you are going to need to learn starting today so you will be able to recognize a deal when you see it because that is really the key. Research the local real estate market in which you plan on investing. This knowledge will help you spot opportunities others cannot see and make buying decisions quickly. You first will want to track market inventory over time. Find out how many active listings are for sale in the local MLS data, and how many sales typically close each month to determine the supply of homes. Under six-month supply is considered a sellers' market, six-month supply is considered a balanced market, and over six-month supply is considered a buyers' market. You should track this number, but note that it is possible for you to make money in an up or a down market, buyers' market or sellers' market. Other things you may want to track are days on the market, median price of a home, and foreclosure rates. Over time, you want to look at trending areas, and price points by neighborhoods. One of the things I do as a broker is a lot of market research which has been invaluable to me and to my clients. Being full time in the real estate business is an advantage to me as an investor because realtors have access to a lot of tools that help us stay on top of what is happening in our local market. Part of my job in working with buyers and sellers is being able to advise my clients about current market value. This is very specialized knowledge that takes into account local market trends, area amenities, schools, and housing availability in various areas of the community.

There are lots of factors that go into choosing housing besides just the amenities in the house itself, and as investors, the more you know the better. Have a network of others you can turn to for advice when you are unsure about something.

Okay, so you have studied the market and different neighborhoods you think you want to focus on. How do you go about finding properties that might work for your deals? There are two main ways I find properties. One is off market pre-foreclosure properties. It is fairly easy to get a list of properties that are in pre-foreclosure in our area, and I am certain you can find them in any area. One source you can use to familiarize yourself with the foreclosure laws in your state is on the web at http://www.realtytrac.com/real-estate-guides/foreclosure-laws. In most areas, you should be able to go online or to your local county government offices and look for them. In Florida and other judicial states, the document you are looking for is called a "Lis Pendens." In some other states, it may be called a "Notice of Default."

Even easier than looking up the info in public records is to subscribe to a service that actually compiles this information and sells it to investors, or sign up for a site like RealtyTrac®, which is the one I use. With RealtyTrac®, for a small monthly fee, you can search pre-foreclosures and foreclosures by zip codes. You can look up specific addresses, and it will give you information similar to what is in the tables below.

RealtyTrac®

Foreclosure Status: **Pre-foreclosure as of 3/29/2016**

Listing Status: **Pre-market**

Loan Details: **1 for $144,130**

Equity/LTV: **-$44,130/144.13%**

Occupancy Status: **Owner occupied**

Property Tax (2015): **$811 (0.94 %)**

Building Permits: **7 Found**

Local Schools: **Above average (B-)**

Crime Rate: **Moderate (B-)**

Criminal Sex Offenders: **8 found within 1 mile**

Drug Labs: **0 found within 1 mile**

Environmental Risks: **29 found within 1 mile**

Flood Risk: **Minimal**

Foreclosure Status:	Pre-foreclosure (Lis Pendens)
Recording Date:	03/29/2016
Entered Date:	04/26/2016
Original Loan Amount:	$144,130
Document Number:	6394/1917
Case Number:	2016CA000416
Related Doc:	1997390446
Related Book Page:	6394/1917

In addition to this data, you can also search for comparable properties, market info and stats and trends by zip code. RealtyTrac® is a national database and is really very affordable and user friendly, and I have been using it for several years now. Note in the case above, it says there is negative equity (-$44,130) and the original loan amount was $144,130 that means the property is most likely not worth more than $100,000. If you want to make an offer on the home, this does present additional challenges, but many investors including myself have profited handsomely from contracting with the seller and negotiating what we call a "short sale." In the example above, one of the key things it tells us is that the property is owner occupied; that means if you are interested in this property, you can mail them something and/or go to the house and see if you can find someone at home. If not, leave them your contact information and offer to help them with their foreclosure by buying the house before that happens. You can also look up the case on the public records and find the attorney who is representing the ban in the foreclosure action. There is a lot of extra paperwork that will be required and the process can take several months, so although it is called a "short-sale," the name was given because in a short sale the bank agrees to accept less than the amount owed. This will perhaps be the longest and most frustrating negotiation, and if you don't have much experience, you may want to seek out an attorney and/or real estate agent that specializes in doing these types of sales. Have the agent list the home then put it under contract: the bank will actually pay a real estate fee if your offer is accepted. The seller will be required to complete a lot of paperwork for the bank including sending them financial information such as tax returns and bank statements as well as a "hardship letter." If the bank determines the seller does not have a legitimate hardship and could afford to keep on paying for the house, the deal could fall through, so get to know the seller and find out why he got behind in the first place. Things like loss of employment, divorce or death of a spouse, job transfer to another part of the country could all qualify as hardships in the right circumstances.

Pre-foreclosure owners are some of the most motivated individuals you will work with, and they can provide you with a steady source of good deals. I learned to do short sale negotiations when it was necessary to help clients who needed to sell and owed too much. When the real estate market crash began in 2007, my real estate company already was managing over 450 rental homes and several homeowners' associations, so my clients were calling me for solutions. Many of my clients were like the people in the above example: they bought when the market was lower and when the market was good they refinanced their property and took out the equity, sometimes to buy more real estate or to pay off credit card or high interest rate debt. Others just bought at the height of the market, and some not only paid more than they should have but also had bad loans that had been given at a teaser rate when the rate adjusted upward. They just could not afford the payments and got behind. Others lost their jobs. There were double the usual number of homes on the market for sale at the time, and prices were dropping. Some of my clients were military or found jobs elsewhere and became landlords when they were unable to sell in a timely manner and needed to do something to pay the mortgage; then later, when the property taxes went up and the homeowners' insurance rates rose and, after a few tenants, the place needed to be painted or carpets changed out or the air conditioning unit broke down, they were faced with a negative situation that was causing them financial hardship. They either stopped making payments and lost the home to foreclosure or learned that there was another option called short sale.

Short sale - a sale of real estate in which the net proceeds from selling the property will fall short of the debts secured by liens against the property

---

When considering the likelihood of success of getting bank approval for a short sale on a given property, you first must have a title search to determine all liens that are currently against the property. These liens can include not only first mortgages but second mortgages, home equity lines of credit (HELOC), IRS liens, mechanics liens *(for unpaid work by contractors, subcontractors, laborers, or material suppliers),* homeowner association liens for unpaid dues, and local property taxes. All lien holders must be contacted and a release obtained or the deal will not be able to close with clear title. I checked the data for Pensacola MLS regarding short sales that were listed since January 1, 2015, and of the 325 properties that were listed as a short sale, 102 are sold and closed, 44 are active now, 65 are currently under contract waiting on bank approval, leaving 114 that either did not sell or had an offer that fell through and never closed and they were removed from the market, either because the seller got tired of trying or they actually got foreclosed. I had a buyer who contracted me earlier this year to try to buy a property that was listed as a short sale. We were waiting on an answer from the seller's lender, when one day, with no real advance warning, we learned the house was sold at the foreclosure auction at the county courthouse, so we had to look for a different one. It isn't always cut and dried.

If you work with a seller that may be a candidate for a short sale, you should advise them to seek both legal and tax advice regarding their specific situation, as there may be legal, tax, and credit ramifications for the seller. In general, it is usually better for a seller to cooperate with a short sale than to let the property go into foreclosure, but each situation is unique.

One of the best deals I ever was involved in that occurred was a short sale that came to me when a client, who was not local but had grown up in Pensacola, called me and asked me to go and look at a condo for him that he was interested in. The condo was in the Perdido area of Escambia County, off Gulf Beach Hwy, located on the ninth floor with a breathtaking view of the intra-coastal waterway; however, I could barely stand to be inside the unit because of the smell from the mold that was growing inside the unit. I took pictures of the unit and called my client. He was very disappointed because it was his intention to get a loan to pay for the condo, and he had no way to supervise and pay for mold remediation, so he said he would have to pass on the unit.

Being a realtor can sometimes make you feel just a little guilty about seeing a good deal, but when he said he was not interested I immediately asked him if he had a problem with me making an offer on the condo for myself. My research told me another property in the same area had recently sold for $115,000 and that someone had paid $421,200 for this unit in January of 2007, just before the market started to tank. It was listed for sale as a short sale

Brantley

for $115,000. Due to the mold and the uncertainty about how much worse it could get while we were waiting on short sale approval, I offered $105,000. After all, I had written into the contract an inspection period to end ten days after the acceptance of the offer by the bank. It took a little longer than I had anticipated because not only was it a short sale but the seller had filed bankruptcy which complicated things a little more. Four months later, I closed on this beautiful condo for a purchase price of $105,000! The mold remediation turned out to be less extensive than I had originally thought, and I ended up spending a little less than $10,000 to get the condo ready for occupancy.

I kept it and enjoyed it on weekends, did some short term renting, and then I sold it for a huge profit one year later. I listed it for $159,900 but actually sold the condo for $151,200 and sold the garage space separately for $22,500. The person who bought the condo is an agent who was working for me at the time, so the commission was taken off the purchase price, and he paid closing. My profit on the sale of the garage and the condo was over $60,000! That was 2 1/2 years ago, and today, that same condo in that complex is worth about $225,000.

This example brings up a good point that is crucial to your long-term success as a real estate investor. Let's talk about factors that affect pricing and desirability of any given property in your town or mine. Obviously, a growing or declining population has an effect on prices; however, not just the population numbers but the demographics are important. Check census data in your area because things like age, income, family size, and the education level of the population is going to tell you a lot about housing trends, size of home, and where people will want to live. Families want to live where there are good schools; they want to be within reasonable commute to their jobs. An example right now in Pensacola, Florida, is the huge expansion going on in the northwestern part of Escambia County because of the Navy Federal Credit Union purchasing and building a call center that is employing thousands. This area was previously "the country." I lived there back in the late '80s and had acreage, a nice house, almost no neighbors, and no traffic. Now, all that has changed, and there are some of the nicest new housing developments cropping up everywhere to accommodate the influx of people.

When jobs are lost or a huge recession occurs, which happened nationally in 2008, prices, especially higher priced real estate, will see a drop. Although there are deals available in every market, sometimes the deals are better than others. Investors should always be educating themselves and should keep their fingers on the pulse of the real estate market. The long-term goal of an investor is to buy when it is hard to sell, and then sell when everyone else wants to buy! You may also want to consider a different plan for different stages in your life.

There is nothing that can accurately predict what the real estate market will do over time. You need to know the fundamentals of a property and try to understand how your properties and investments will be impacted by changes in the market, both good and bad.

While wholesaling, rehabbing, and flipping are all great ways to make money in real estate pretty quickly, overall, I have always looked at real estate as a long-term investment where passive income starts to compound. Long-term investing in real estate allows you to take advantage of appreciation and leverage while you are building passive income. I believe if you want to achieve financial freedom through real estate, you must buy properties and hold on to them for the long term. Whatever your income goal is, it can be achieved through the cash flow from your real estate investments; you just have to take the time to grow your portfolio.

You may choose your own investment criteria, and it may be different from mine, but I am going to tell you from years of investing and property management what works for me, and some things that I have learned from years of doing it. I am going to tell you what properties I, personally, believe are best to use for long-term rentals. You are not going to use the same criteria for something you intend to hold on to as you would for something you plan to wholesale or flip because you are planning to keep this and keep it generating income. In general, the larger, more expensive homes will not generate as much cash flow for you as the smaller bread and butter homes, but I suggest you do not compromise on location; buy a smaller home in the best location you can afford that will give you consistent cash flow.

Criteria I look for are three bedrooms and two baths, public sewer, no flood insurance required, no pool. A garage is nice, but I will buy homes without one. A fenced yard is a bonus, and if there is not one I usually go ahead and fence it because tenants and resale buyers in our area prefer homes that are fenced. If it does not meet my criteria, does that mean I won't buy it? Not necessarily. I evaluate each deal, maybe I am not crazy about buying and holding a particular property, but because the price is so low, I determine I can buy it to flip and make a nice profit.

I always check school and crime data which is very important. The old saying "location, location, location" is very appropriate. If you want to hold for long term and get the benefit of cash flow plus appreciation, the location should be one of your biggest concerns. You can fix cosmetic issues, but you cannot move the property. One last important thing for long-term investing is that I do not buy houses in neighborhoods where the surrounding homes are owned almost entirely by landlords. I recommend you do the same, and look for properties in neighborhoods with mostly owner occupants and fewer landlords. In my area, you can go to the local property appraisers' site and look up a subdivision by name, and it will actually give you the option of print mailing labels. So if you have a subdivision of 100 homes, for example, and over 50% of the mailing labels show the owners' mailing addresses are not the same as the property addresses, that's an indication that there are too many renters in the area.

Neighborhoods change over time. You can l earn to anticipate future trends by doing research and studying the neighborhoods. Past sales data is now available to the public online through county sites. You can also talk to neighbors; they can give you a lot of information about the number of renters in the area, as well as to the homeowners. Be sure to give them your information, as it may come in handy to be friends with the neighbors if you decide to buy the home after completing your research.

One area that this is of particular concern is when buying condominiums. Most lenders have underwriting guidelines, and FHA, VA, and Fannie Mae have underwriting criteria that say they will not give a loan on a property that has too many renters. In my experience, that number usually falls between 35-50%, so loans on condos that don't meet these requirements would be difficult to obtain. When we get into the property management section, there will be lots more real-life stories l encountered, both in my personal investments and those we manage for others; and my advice is to stay away from the high crime areas of the city, look for properties in the best location you can afford to buy in where over 50% are owner occupants, and pay particular attention to the people living in the homes close by the home you are looking at and how well these homes are kept, how many are owner and how many are tenant occupied. Make these steps part of your discovery process when looking for potential homes to make offers on.

If you want to hold for the long term and get the benefit of cash flow plus appreciation, the location should be one of your biggest concerns. You can fix cosmetic issues but you cannot move the property.

You also want to look at the price, the cost of homeowner's insurance and taxes, the potential current market rent, and number of days expected on the market before you can start collecting rent!

Find a good lender and a good real estate agent. DO NOT use an agent that has never owned a home, much less have any experience with rentals, because they cannot possibly know how to advise you on these properties. You are looking for bargains that have really good bones and a good location, but you cannot be as picky about things like the appliances or the floorcoverings as you would if you were buying it as a consumer. Remember: this is an investment, and you are an investor. If you don't like it and the price is right, you just need to know how much it is going to cost to change it. You do not have to live in this house, but you need to be able to rent it.

Once you find an agent you can work with, have them run comps, advise you about offers, and listen to their advice. If you don't want to take their advice, then you may need to find another agent or you need to learn it all yourself. I recommend you get started with the purchase of your first investment property. Get the advice of an agent for any uncertainties.

Chapter 4 Summary

→ Wholesaling, rehabbing, flipping, and buy-and-hold are basic strategies used to build wealth using real estate.

→ The types of properties that you should be considering for your investments are usually distress sales of some kind such as pre-foreclosures, short sales, foreclosures, bank or government owned homes. You can find these properties through networking, online sources, and even the local Multiple Listing Service.

→ Research and educate yourself on the areas you are considering buying in, and decide what criteria you will use to select the homes.

→ Develop a team with a few good lenders, real estate agents, insurance agents, and title agents available to network with and learn from, as well as use their professional services.

Chapter 5

Types of Ownership, Financing, Title, and the Closing Process

The following section outlines some of the different types of ownership structures you can choose to hold your real estate in.

Sole Proprietorship- individual ownership: you are fully responsible and personally liable for the property. As a result, all of your personal assets could be attacked if a renter filed a lawsuit against you. If you decide to form a business as a sole proprietorship, you either use your name or you must register a "doing business as" (DBA) with the state.

Partnership- an association of two or more persons to carry on as co-owners of a business for profit. You and your partners determine in advance based on money and services contributed what percentage each of you owns. Your ownership percentage will determine your liability or responsibility if a lawsuit is brought against the partnership. Before entering into a partnership, you should have full knowledge of the credit and legal history of your potential partners.

Corporation- This type of ownership gives you the best protection from liability but takes a lot more work to set up and manage. In the eyes of the IRS and the law, you and your corporation are different entities. That means you will need to complete two tax returns each year at tax time. You also need to elect officers and directors, keep corporate books, and hold at least one annual meeting.

Limited Liability Company (LLC) - a business structure that combines the pass-through taxation of a partnership or sole proprietorship with the limited liability of a corporation. It is a separate entity, and you can have a separate bank account, but you can file one tax return between both you and the LLC, just like with a partnership. One thing to keep in mind is that once you establish an LLC as a business entity, you will be required to use an attorney in all legal matters including tenant evictions. If there were a lawsuit involving a property held in an LLC, you would need attorney representation, but the most you would be liable for would be the amount of the LLC's assets.

Trust - the legal relationship between one person, the trustee, having an equitable ownership or management of certain property and another person, the beneficiary, owning the legal title to that property. Most trusts are founded by the persons (called trustors, settlors and/or donors) who execute a written declaration of trust which establishes the trust and spells out the terms and conditions upon which it will be conducted. The declaration names the original trustee or trustees, successor trustees ro means to choose future turstees. The assets of the trust are usually given to the trust by the creators, although assets may be added by others. During the life of the trust, profits and, sometimes, a portion of the principal, may be distributed to the beneficiaries; and the remainder is usually distributed upon the occurrence of an event such as the death of the creator. A trust may be created as an alternative to a will in order to avoid probate and higher taxation. There are many types of trusts, including "revocable trusts," created to handle the trustors' assets (with the trustor acting as initial trustee), also called a "living trust," "irrevocable trusts," which cannot be changed at any time; and "charitable remainder trusts," which provide for the eventual guaranteed distribution of the assets to charity, providing a substantial tax benefit.

Individual Retirement Account- The asset purchased would be titled in the name of your IRA. This is a tax-deferred way to purchase and sell real estate and will be discussed more in the next chapter.

Once you have decided how you want to take title to the real estate you plan to purchase, you will need to look into how you plan to pay for your real estate. A mortgage is a loan that helps you pay for your real estate purchase. I am going to tell you up front that the loan process can be very frustrating, but this is another area you must educate yourself about and interview your potential lenders because you do not want too many lenders out there pulling your credit while shopping for your loan as this could lower your credit score, and your interest rate and approval will depend on that. Do not give them your social security number or permission to pull your credit report until you are pretty sure this is the lender you plan to deal with.

I recommend you choose a local lender. Someone that acts as a broker or correspondent lender usually has more than one option for submitting your loan.

Mortgage Broker- an intermediary who brokers mortgage loans on behalf of individuals.

Mortgage Lender or Mortgage Banker - a company, individual or institution that originates mortgages. Mortgage bankers use their own funds, or funds borrowed from a warehouse lender, to fund mortgages.

Correspondent Lender- the origination and sale of mortgages on the "mortgage secondary market," where mortgage originators and mortgage investors get together to do business.

A local bank or credit union relationship may also be beneficial, but you should interview your loan officer and find out how many loans they can get for you under their guidelines. Fannie Mae allows 10 loans for investors, but not all lenders are willing to allow investors to have that many loans, and if they do, there may be stricter requirements. In our area, there are some local credit unions and banks that keep some loans as what they call portfolio loans: these loans typically are going to have different interest rates and terms than a standard Fannie Mae product, but they can be beneficial in certain situations.

Following is an explanation of the typical loans you would be using to purchase long-term investment property.

Loans underwritten according to Fannie Mae guidelines: the Federal National Mortgage Association aka **Fannie Mae,** *is a quasi-government organization that was created to purchase mortgage loans from the primary lenders. In order to be purchased by Fannie Mae, lenders must make sure the borrowers and the loan products meet strict underwriting guidelines.*

Portfolio Loans- *loans held by an investment bank because they do not meet the qualifications of secondary market underwriters like Fannie Mae*

For most conventional financing, you will need the following documentation:

→ Two years' tax returns

→ Most recent two months' bank statements

→ Copies of the info on any investment properties you already own to include existing leases, copies of homeowner's insurance policies, tax bills, and a recent mortgage statement from the lender

Note: If you have not owned the property long enough to have it show up on your latest income tax return, don't count on them using the rent to qualify you. If you have income from self-employment or real estate investments and it is not W2 income, they will not count that unless you have two years in that business.

In order to get started in buying long-term investment properties, you are going to have to qualify based on the income from your current employment, so I suggest you look at your credit situation and start paying off your cars, credit cards, etc. and get your debt ratio down to a minimum before you even start this process. If you have a credit card with reasonable interest rate or the potential for a large cash advance you may be able to use that for part of your down payment, but again, your debt ratio must be in line or you will not get financed. You will need 20% down for a typical, standard, conventional investor loan; the interest rate will be slightly higher than if it were owner occupied. And in some cases, the lender may require 25% down, especially if the property is a condominium. **Do your homework before you apply!**

Mortgage Choice

We also need to pay close attention to the current interest rate environment when we do our financing. Paying cash is not always the best, and there are different times when a 15-year mortgage works better than a 30-year mortgage and vice versa.

There is always a cost to use money. Even when we pay cash, we lose the earnings ability of those dollars, and that is called "lost opportunity cost."

Here are some very basic examples so that you can understand that each situation needs to be measured based on the best information at the time:

Cash flow with all debt rates and earning rates equal at 4%. Note: even though if you save over $38,000 in interest doing the 15-year, you don't really save any money if you took the cash flow difference and invested it at the earnings rate. Think of it like this from a cash flow perspective: pay off the 15-year and invest the P&I payment of $739.69 at 4% for 15-years (30-year time frame - 15 years to payoff mortgage and 15 years investing) you end up with $182,000 saved up. If you take the cash flow difference of $262 per month and invested it for the full 30 years while not paying the 30-year mortgage, you end up with $182,000 saved up. They are the same! The interest difference was not the only factor in the mortgage choice.

Mortgage Choice

	Cash	Mortgage 1	Mortgage 2
Federal Tax Bracket:	0.00%		
Net Earnings Potential:	4.00%		
Illustration Period: 360	360		
	Cash	Mortgage 1	Mortgage 2
(Cash=Value of Home) Principal:	$100,000	$100,000	$100,000
Down Payment:		$0	$0
Interest Rate:		4.00%	4.00%
No. of Payments:		180	360
Payment:		$739.69	$477.42
Additional Payment:		$0	$0
New Payoff Month:		180	360
***Interest Only Payment:		$333	$333
Cumulative Interest:		-$33,141	-$71,870
Illustration Period Adjustment:		$182,030	$0
Future Value of Payment Margin:			$182,030

Home Appreciation	
Tax . CG Rate:	15.00%
Growth Rate:	0.00 %
Tax Exemption:	$0
Future Value:	$100,000
Capital Gains Tax:	$0

$262:	Monthly Difference To Invest @ 4%

Mortgage 2 vs Mortgage 1:	
	$0

DISCLAIMER: The information provided by these calculators is for illustrative purposes only. The information entered may vary from your actual loan, mortgage, investment, or savings results. Interest rates are hypothetical and are not meant to represent a specific investment. Rates of return will vary over time, particularly for long-term investments. They do not include consideration of the time value of money, inflation, an fluctuation in principal or in many instances, taxes. Past performance is not a guarantee of future results. Material discussed is meant for general illustration and/or informational purposes only and it is not to be construed as tax, legal, or investment advice. The calculated results are not guaranteed to be accurate and are in no way endorsed, offered or guaranteed to DLA.

Wait a minute - isn't the rate lower on a 15-year mortgage? Yep, usually. So let's look at that.

In this scenario, the 15-year mathematically is better. But what about risk to cash flow? What about the opportunity to earn more than 4% in a side account or alternative investment? What about tax deductions? These are just a few!

Mortgage Choice

	Cash	Mortgage 1	Mortgage 2
Federal Tax Bracket:	0.00%		
Net Earnings Potential:	4.00%		
Illustration Period: 360	360		
	Cash	Mortgage 1	Mortgage 2
(Cash=Value of Home) Principal:	$100,000	$100,000	$100,000
Down Payment:		$0	$0
Interest Rate:		3.50%	4.00%
No. of Payments:		180	360
Payment:		$714.88	$477.42
Additional Payment:		$0	$0
New Payoff Month:		180	360
***Interest Only Payment:		$292	$333
Cumulative Interest:		-$28,677	-$71,870
Illustration Period Adjustment:		$175,926	$0
Future Value of Payment Margin:			$164,814

Home Appreciation	
Tax . CG Rate:	15.00%
Growth Rate:	0.00 %
Tax Exemption:	$0
Future Value:	$100,000
Capital Gains Tax:	$0

$237:	Monthly Difference
	To Invest @ 4%

Mortgage 2 vs Mortgage 1: $0
-11,112

Let's take the scenario above and add a tax deduction.
Now the 30-year looks better!

We could run hundreds of scenarios. But here is the point
being made: you need to measure your property investment
idea and you need to measure your particular mortgage or
financing situation to see what is best for your circumstances
and beliefs.

Mortgage Choice

	Cash	Mortgage 1	Mortgage 2		
Federal Tax Bracket:	28.00%			Home Appreciation	
Net Earnings Potential:	4.00%			Tax . CG Rate:	15.00%
Illustration Period: 360	360			Growth Rate:	0.00 %
(Cash=Value of Home) Principal:	$100,000	$100,000	$100,000	Tax Exemption:	$0
Down Payment:		$0	$0	Future Value:	$100,000
Interest Rate:		3.50%	4.00%	Capital Gains Tax:	$0
No. of Payments:		180	360		
Payment:		$714.88	$477.42	$237:	Monthly Difference
Additional Payment:		$0	$0		To Invest @ 4%
New Payoff Month:		180	360		
***Interest Only Payment:		$292	$333		
Cumulative Interest:		-$28,677	-$71,870		
Illustration Period Adjustment:		$175,926	$0	Mortgage 2 vs Mortgage 1:	
Future Value of Payment Margin:			$164,814	11,923	

Private financing may be available in the form of seller-held note and mortgage, land contracts, or other private money. Banks typically have a lower cost of funds than other lenders. Depositors keep a lot of money in their checking and savings accounts. Thus, banks have easy access to those funds to lend out. And if banks don't pay interest for those deposits or pay very little interest like they do today (under ½ percent) – then those funds are very cheap for the bank to use. Private money will typically carry higher interest rates, and they may require balloon payments. Be very careful when you look into private financing, and make sure you know what you are getting.

Another type of lender is called a hard-money lender. These lenders typically charge points plus a high interest rate because they are funding deals that do not conform to bank standards; however, there are situations where, if the deal is good enough and you need this as a short-term solution, it could work; just know that it is going to cost you. Most people use hard-money loans to buy properties that need extensive rehab and that they plan to flip because they are normally short-term. Six months to up to two years are the terms for this type of transaction. This may be the only way to fund the purchase and rehab of a property that is in need of extensive repairs, and they will lend money not only for the purchase but for the rehab. This portion of the funding is typically taken in draws against the work being performed; draws and payments will be paid as work is completed.

Hard-money lenders will typically lend based up to 65-70% of the ARV (After Repair Value), and they typically charge 3-5% of the loan amount upfront with interest rates between 12 and 18%. They charge interest monthly with a balloon payment of the principal balance due at the end of the term. With this type of loan product, although it can be beneficial if you need the money for your project, you really need to shop around for the best deal before taking the plunge into one of these loans. Make sure you are getting the best deal available, and again, I suggest trying to find a local lender who does these types of loans.

Another type of financing is called transactional funding. These are extremely short-term loans. They can be used if you are wholesaling a property, have a buyer lined up to purchase, but need to close on the deal first before transferring title. If you are contracting on foreclosures, there is typically a clause most banks put in the contract that says the contract is not assignable, so the only way to wholesale these is to have a back-to-back closing, and you cannot have a closing without cash in the form of certified funds and a title transferred into your name before you can sell it to someone else. Transactional funding works well in these cases, but it will cost you some of your profit to use this type of funding. Transactional lenders will most likely not require an appraisal, credit check, or income verification—the funding is based solely on you having an end buyer already in place—and they typically won't release the funds for these transactions unless the end buyer is cleared to close. Most transactional lenders will charge 2-3 points upfront (2-3% of the loan amount) and from

12-15% interest. If the deal you have is profitable enough to offset the risk and costs involved, having this type of lender on your real estate team is really important.

 Once you get your lender lined up, you will need to get a preapproval letter from them before you start making offers. This will ensure that your offer gets considered, especially when dealing with bank-owned properties and short sales. Most banks will not even look at an offer with a financing contingency unless it is accompanied by a preapproval letter.

Now you are ready to make offers. If you are dealing with properties that are listed on the local multiple listing service, you should have a good real estate agent on your team that is willing to work with you. Many say go to the listing agent. As a broker who has represented lots of buyers in transactions, I do not think the listing agent is always looking out for your best interest, as they represent the seller in the transaction and conflicts can arise. You do not get a better deal by going to the listing agent; usually, they make twice as much money because they do not have to share their commission with a buyer's agent. Many banks and mortgage lenders, as well as VA and HUD, have their own special contracts and addendums that need to be signed if you hope to get the property. Your agent will be able to help you make sure you submit the correct paperwork. If you are buying something that is "by owner," you should have some type of standard contract you can use for that purpose. If you are using financing, be sure your contract has contingency clauses for both an inspection period and financing. Below is a sample inspection contingency clause:

PROPERTY INSPECTIONS AND RIGHT TO CANCEL: Buyer shall have 10 days after Effective Date ("Inspection Period") within which to have such inspections of the Property performed as Buyer shall desire during the Inspection Period. If Buyer determines, in Buyer's sole discretion, that the Property is not acceptable to Buyer, Buyer may terminate this Contract by delivering written notice of such election to Seller prior to expiration of Inspection Period. If Buyer timely terminates this Contract, the Deposit paid shall be returned to Buyer; thereupon, Buyer and Seller shall be released of all further obligations under this Contract; however, Buyer shall be responsible for prompt payment for such inspections, for repair of damage to, and restoration of, the Property resulting from such inspections, and shall provide Seller with paid receipts for all work done on the Property (the preceding provision shall survive termination of this Contract). Unless Buyer exercises the right to terminate granted herein, Buyer accepts the physical condition of the Property and any violation of governmental, building, environmental, and safety codes, restrictions, or requirements, but subject to Seller's continuing AS IS Maintenance Requirement, and Buyer shall be responsible for any and all repairs and improvements required by Buyer's lender.

In my experience, you will start evaluating properties by looking at the online pictures and data that is available in public records. You can use projection of income and expenses and determine if the numbers look favorable. You can use something similar to the figures in the investment analysis I included in Chapter Two. When you are making your projections, you will first need to determine the expected rent you can get for the property, and then subtract the typical expenses such as property taxes, homeowner's insurance, monthly mortgage note payments, as well as a projected amount for maintenance and repairs as well as professional management services. Although many people hold the tenant responsible for minor repairs in the lease agreement, you should consider holding back 5-10% of the monthly rent in a fund dedicated to a reserve for future maintenance and repairs. If not needed it would be a nice savings but you never know when the air conditioner will stop working and need to be replaced, so you have to be ready to maintain your property and know that you can still have a monthly cash flow. If the online data and the projections you calculate are favorable, you may end up viewing five to ten properties and making offers on five or more to get one property under contract, and even then, it could fall through due to a bad inspection report. When negotiating, you need to know that when the deal is good enough: a good buyer knows when to quit negotiating and buy. You will want to build some profit into the monthly cash flow, just what rate of turn is acceptable to you depending on the risk you are willing to take. When banks put foreclosed homes on the sale market and start marketing, they usually put them at what they call the "quick sale" price, which often means they are already a "good deal." Don't lose out on a good deal because you are not willing to pay the asking price or above. There are many different ways to get these deals, and some of them you only get one shot to make an offer: don't automatically assume you will get a second chance to negotiate the price because that may not happen.

There are other factors that can affect your probability of getting your offer accepted when you are dealing with multiple offer scenarios that are common when bank owned properties are being sold. Things you can do to make your offer look better than the next offer are shorten the inspection period, offer a higher deposit, offer all cash with no financing contingency, or even meet your inspector there in advance of making the offer and make the offer cash with no contingencies. This is where having a good real estate agent, familiar with working with investment properties can really help you; they most likely have had other dealings with the listing agent and know what contract forms to use and how to get the offer submitted with the proper documentation. Another thing you should do is consider leaving your offer in as a backup if it is not the winning bid. Many times, deals go south and fall through, and you might be second in line and willing to move forward.

Once you negotiate an offer and it has been accepted by the seller, be sure to follow the timelines that have been set up in the contract for getting your inspections done. Inspections are not only for your protection but may also be required by your insurance carrier just to get accurate quotes. This is especially true in Florida, where I buy and sell property. There are several types of inspections required in the state of Florida because of the difficulty with getting homeowners' insurance. Be sure to get everything you need, and make sure you are happy with the findings and can get insurance on the property at a reasonable rate before the inspection deadline. Do not forget a termite inspection. In some areas, termites can be a huge problem that can cause thousands of dollars in damage to the house, some of which may be hidden between the walls or under the house. Stucco homes that have not been properly maintained can have cracks and defects that can allow moisture to get into the walls, which can also cause additional damage. It is also advisable to get one of your contractors to meet with the inspector and put together an estimate of the cost to correct the defects found by the home inspector and any other items you want done to the home before you rent it out. You can use the estimates to renegotiate the price or ask for repairs to be done.

In Florida, if the home is over 30 years old, generally, you will need a wind mitigation inspection and a four-point inspection just to get accurate insurance quotes; and if the property is in a flood zone, you will something called a flood elevation certificate, which is a document your insurance company will need to determine the cost of the flood insurance for a property located in a special flood hazard area. A licensed surveyor will need to be engaged to perform the evaluation required in order to issue the elevation certificate.

Because of the wide variation in the cost of flood and homeowner's insurance in some parts of Florida, you may consider adding an additional contingency to the contract that states you will not be obligated to purchase the home if the insurance will cost more than a designated amount you feel you are willing to pay based on your income projections.

Once you have determined that you are satisfied with all inspections, you need to make sure your lender is aware of the timeline you have for closing so that if anything comes up and your loan gets turned down you will be able to get out of the contract based on the last contingency you should have which is the financing contingency. Things that your lender will most likely require in addition to your income and assets documentation and property appraisal are a clear title report and a recent boundary survey of the property. Once all these things are completed and the loan has gone through final underwriting, you will be ready to go to closing.

Please note that the closing date is something that is typically negotiated by buyer and seller as part of the initial contract between the parties, and time is of the essence. This date can be a fixed date or an on-or-before date. If it needs to be changed or extended all parties will need to agree to the change and sign a contract amendment. Some banks and federal institutions, such as FHA and VA, have strict guidelines on how far in advance they must receive the paperwork so it can be reviewed and signed off on, so you should keep your lender and the title company in the loop and informed about the particulars of the seller of the property.

property. I suggest you use a local real estate attorney or title office you like to work with, and make sure they and your lender are in communication early on, as well as the seller, so this can go smoothly.

Chapter 5 Summary

Before going to contract on a property, you need to decide how you will be taking title to the property and, if financing is involved, how you will finance it. You should have a pre-approval letter to give you credibility with the seller. If you want your offer to be taken seriously, don't wait until you find the right property to get your financing arranged. Once you have an accepted contract, get all required inspections including property inspection, wind and 4-point inspections, stucco inspection, termite inspection, and any other inspections you want or the basic home inspector recommends. If there are items you are concerned about, get your contractor to meet with the inspector and give you an estimate of the cost to correct any problems that are found. You should also have a relationship with a local real estate attorney or title company that can issue title insurance and close the transaction.

Chapter 6
Tax-Advantaged
Investing Strategies

When you are investing in real estate, remember that for short-term investments, your tax rate is going to be basically the same as ordinary income tax, and the investments will most likely be taxed at your highest tax bracket. You are most likely going to be required to pay quarterly estimated taxes to avoid IRS penalties and problems coming up with the money for taxes at the end of the year.

Example: Let's say you profit $20,000 on a flip that you only held for 6 months. Based on your other income plus this you are in the 28% tax bracket. $20,000 x 28% = $5600. If you close in August 2016, you should be prepared to send the IRS $5600 for the third quarter. This money is due to be postmarked by September.

That being said, there are some vehicles that can be used to invest that are tax advantaged. One thing I highly recommend if you are young and starting out is to take advantage of the tax benefit of selling and replacing your personal residence every couple of years. This is one way to pay no income tax. When I first started buying real estate,

I used this IRS rule several times. Remember when you are buying your personal residence that it is an investment; look for a great buy in the best location that needs a little updating or a remodel, and you can build equity fast enough to make it worthwhile to sell it in two years, pay no taxes on the gain, and do it again every couple of years.

There are three criteria the IRS uses in order to determine if you qualify for special tax exemption or the sale of your personal residence:

→   For the two years prior to the date of sale, you did not exclude gain from the sale of another home.

→   During the five years prior to the date of sale, you owned the home for at least two years.

→   During the five years prior to the date of sale, you lived in the home as your main home for at least two years.

Note: To meet the second and third requirements, the two-year time periods do not necessarily have to be made up of 24 consecutive months. For married couples filing jointly, a $500,000 maximum exclusion is available if both spouses meet the first and third requirements and at least one spouse meets the second requirement.

If the market has not gone up enough to make it worth selling, consider turning your residence into a rental property and purchasing a new personal residence. The advantage to this is you are taking advantage of better interest rates and a lower down payment is required to buy a personal residence. After living there one to two years, you turn that into a rental and get another loan with a lower down payment and interest rate. This is making the most of the concept of leverage.

There are two types of taxable gains you need to be aware of when selling any type of investment including stocks or real estate:

Short-Term Capital Gain is profit on investments held for less than 1 year. These investments are taxed the same as ordinary income you get from your regular job. Because of the way the tax tables are set up, they will be taxed at the highest marginal tax rate. The amount that is subject to income tax will be determined by calculating your basis in the property which is usually what you paid unless you have claimed depreciation or done extensive renovations which will affect your cost basis, and subtracting that from the sales price minus the expenses of sale.

Long-Term Capital Gain is profit resulting from an investment held for at least a year. Long-term capital gains are taxed differently than short-term gains. As of the time of book publishing, any long-term capital gains that fall in the highest tax bracket (39.6%) will be taxed at a rate of just 20%, any long-term capital gains that fall in the 25-35% tax brackets will be taxed at a rate of just 15%, and any long-term capital gains that fall in the 10% or 15% tax brackets will not be taxed at all. You should check with your CPA for tax law updates, as these rates have been known to change over the years; but in general, if there is likely to be a large profit on the sale of a piece of real estate, you will get preferential tax treatment if you hold on to the property at least a year before selling.

An important takeaway here is that if you're ever considering selling an investment that has increased in value, it might be a good idea to think about holding the asset long enough for the long-term capital gain to be considered

Another strategy is a 1031 exchange. Under Section 1031 of the United States Internal Revenue Code (26 U.S.C. § 1031), the exchange of certain types of property may defer the recognition of capital gains or losses due upon sale and allow you to defer any capital gains taxes otherwise due. In 1979, this was expanded by the courts to include non-simultaneous sale and purchase of real estate.

Section 1031 of the Internal Revenue Code (26 U.S.C. § 1031) states the recognition rules for realized gains (or losses) that arise as a result of an exchange of like-kind property held or productive use in trade or business or for investment. It states that none of the realized gain or loss will be recognized at the time of the exchange. When selling a property that has been held for investment, you should first calculate, or have your CPA calculate, what the expected gain is and the amount of taxes you will owe if you sell. Long-term capital gains, which is the tax for real property that has been held for over a year, is taxed at a much lower rate than ordinary income tax; so what you need to remember is you will not avoid payment of the tax entirely. You are just going to defer the payment to a future date.

In the short term, it actually should give you more money to invest in the present, which can help grow your portfolio; but somewhere down the road with very few exceptions, that tax will have to be paid. Many people that do 1031 exchanges are banking on the fact that their tax bracket will be lower in retirement than it is while working. That may or may not be true for everyone, but it can definitely work to rid yourself from an unwanted tax bill and help your rental portfolio to grow faster, because if you don't have to pay taxes upon the sale of an investment property you will have more money to invest now. Everyone likes to tell you that you should use this method because they assume you will be in a lower tax bracket at retirement age. However, keep in mind that if you are truly on the road to financial freedom that may or may not be the case. Also right now, long-term capital gains are taxed at a lower rate than ordinary income; so it is possible that if the tax laws change you could actually end up paying more tax later than you would right now. Before you decide if a 1031 exchange is right for you, get the advice of a good CPA.

Many people are aware of a 1031 exchange but have no idea what it means. You cannot fix a mistake after it has been done, so I am going to provide you with the basics here, and more detail will be provided in appendix B if you need it. Whatever you do, **please get the help of a qualified intermediary and make sure you follow their guidelines exactly to avoid any issues later with the IRS.** It is also helpful to use a real estate agent and a lender that have been trained and have done these types of transactions before.

The following sequence represents the order of steps in a typical 1031 exchange. Greater details can be found in Appendix B.

1. Retain the services of tax counsel/CPA.

2. Sell property A, including the Cooperation Clause in the sales agreement. Make sure your escrow officer/closing agent contacts the Qualified Intermediary to order the exchange documents.

3. Enter into a 1031 exchange agreement with your Qualified Intermediary.

4. The sale closes, and the closing statement reflects that the Qualified Intermediary was the seller, and the proceeds go to your Qualified Intermediary. The funds should be placed in a separate account. The closing date of the relinquished property is Day 0

of the exchange, and that's when the clock begins to tick. Written identification of the address of the replacement property must be sent within 45 days and must be acquired by the taxpayer within 180 days.

5. The taxpayer sends written identification of the address or legal description of the replacement property to the Qualified Intermediary on or before day 45.

6. Taxpayer enters into an agreement to purchase replacement property, again including the Cooperation Clause.

7. When escrow is prepared to close and prior to the 180th day, the Qualified Intermediary forwards the exchange funds and gross proceeds to escrow, and the closing statement reflects the Qualified Intermediary as the buyer.

8. Taxpayer files form 8824 with the IRS when taxes are filed and whatever similar document your particular state requires.

Highlights of the 1031 Exchange

The basis of the new property is the same as the basis of the property given up, minus any money received by the taxpayer, plus any gain (or minus any loss) recognized on the transaction.

Real property outside the United States and real property located in the United States are not like-kind

The sale of the relinquished property and the acquisition of the replacement property do not have to be simultaneous. For a non-simultaneous exchange the taxpayer must use a Qualified Intermediary, follow guidelines of the IRS, and use the proceeds of the sale to buy more qualifying, like-kind investment or business property. The replacement property must be "identified" within 45 days after the sale of the old property, and the acquisition of the replacement property must be completed within 180 days of the sale of the old property.

Section 1031 is most often used in connection with sales of real property. For real property exchanges under Section 1031, any property that is considered "real property" under the law of the state where the property is located will be considered "like-kind" so long as both the old and the new property is held by the owner for investment, or for active use in a trade or business, or for the production of income.

To obtain full benefit, the replacement property must be of equal or greater value and all of the proceeds from the relinquished property must be used to acquire the replacement property.

The taxpayer cannot receive the proceeds of the sale of the old property; this will disqualify the exchange for the portion of the sale proceeds that the taxpayer received. For this reason, exchanges (particularly non-simultaneous changes) are typically structured so that the taxpayer's interest in the relinquished property is assigned to a Qualified Intermediary prior to the close of the sale. In this way, the taxpayer does not have access to or control over the funds when the sale of the old property closes.

At the close of the first property sale, the proceeds are sent by the closing agent (typically a title company, escrow company, or closing attorney) to the Qualified Intermediary, who holds the funds until such time as the transaction for the acquisition of the replacement property is ready to close. Then the proceeds from the sale of the relinquished property are deposited by the Qualified Intermediary to purchase the replacement property. After the acquisition of the replacement property closes, the Qualifying Intermediary delivers the property to the taxpayer, all without the taxpayer ever having receipt of the funds.

The prevailing idea behind the 1031 Exchange is that since the taxpayer is merely exchanging one property for another of "like-kind" there is nothing received by the taxpayer that can be used to pay taxes.

In addition, the taxpayer has continuity of investment by replacing the old property. All gain is still locked up in the exchanged property, so no gain or loss is "recognized" or claimed for income tax purposes.

Although it is not used in the Internal Revenue Code, the term "Boot" is commonly used in discussing the tax implications of a 1031 Exchange. Boot is an old English term meaning "Something given in addition to." "Boot received" is the money or fair market value of "Other Property" received by the taxpayer in an exchange. Money includes all cash equivalents, debts, liabilities or mortgages of the taxpayer assumed by the other party, or liabilities to which the property exchanged by the taxpayer is subject. "Other Property" is property that is non-like-kind such as personal property, a promissory note from the buyer, a promise to perform work on the property, a business, and etc.

There are many ways for a taxpayer to receive boot, even inadvertently. It is important for an exchangor to understand what can result in boot if taxable income is to be avoided.

The most common sources of boot include the following:

Cash boot taken from the exchange. This will usually be in the form of "Net cash received", or the difference between cash received from the sale of the relinquished property and cash paid to acquire the replacement property. Net cash received can result when a taxpayer is "Trading down" in the exchange (i.e. the sale price of replacement property(ies) is less than that of the relinquished.)

Debt reduction boot occurs when a taxpayer's debt on replacement property is less than the debt which was on the relinquished property. As is the case with cash boot, debt reduction boot can occur when a taxpayer is "trading down" in the exchange. Debt reduction can be offset with cash used to purchase the replacement property.

Also, if proceeds from the sale are used to service non-transaction costs at closing the result is the same as if the taxpayer had received cash from the exchange and then used the cash to pay these costs. Taxpayers should bring cash to the closing of the sale of their property to pay for the following: non-transaction costs: i.e. Rent pro-rations, utility escrow charges, tenant damage deposits transferred to the buyer, and any other charges unrelated to the closing.

Borrowing more money than is necessary to close on replacement property will not result in receiving tax-free money from the closing. The funds from the loan will first be applied toward the purchase. If the addition of exchange funds creates a surplus at the closing, all unused exchange funds will be returned to the Qualified Intermediary, presumably to be used to acquire more replacement property.

Loan acquisition costs (origination and other fees related to acquiring the loan) for the replacement property should be brought to the closing from personal funds. Individuals usually take the position that loan acquisition costs are being paid out of the proceeds of the loan. However, the IRS may take the position that these costs are being paid with exchange funds. This position is usually the position of the financing institution, also.

The acquisition of the replacement property closes, and Qualifying Intermediary delivers the property to the taxpayer, all without the taxpayer ever having receipt of the funds.

Self-Directed Retirement Plans to Purchase Real Estate

A self-directed individual retirement arrangement (IRA gives you the freedom and flexibility to choose exactly how to invest your savings. With a self-directed IRA, you can expand and diversify your investment opportunities beyond the stock market, gaining access to a variety of assets, such as mortgages, notes, real estate, precious metals, and private placements, as well as the more typical stocks, bonds, certificates of deposit, and mutual funds.

Self-directed IRAs are most commonly traditional, rollover, or Roth plans. A rollover IRA is something you can do if you are no longer employed with a company but you contributed to a 401 K or other qualified plan while employed. Once you are no longer employed you have the option of leaving that money in the plan or rolling it over into an IRA; that is why it is called a rollover IRA. As with any qualified plan, the important thing if you plan to use these funds, you must not touch the money because that could be considered a distribution. The best way to handle any kind of rollover is for the company you plan to set up your rollover IRA with to request the funds from the company that is currently holding the plan funds.

A traditional or rollover self-directed IRA allows you to invest in real estate tax deferred just like a 1031 Exchange does. All IRAs must have a custodian or trustee to administer account funds. These types of accounts also come with rules and possible expenses, so you should shop around to find a company you feel comfortable with. You can use an account like this to do wholesaling, rehabbing, flipping, own rental property; and you can even do installment sales and seller financing with them, as long as you follow the rules. These assets will then be owned by your IRA, and all the income they generate will accumulate in your account to provide you with income upon retirement. Consult with your tax advisor or financial planner on the best course of action for you and your retirement savings. I, myself, have invested in notes and real estate with my retirement funds, and it has worked out well for me so far.

Your retirement plan is intended to benefit you when you retire, and not a moment before. Transactions that can be interpreted as providing you immediate financial gain, or those that involve "disqualified persons," are not allowed. If your transactions violate the basic intent of your IRA, your account may be subject to penalties. (See IRS Section 4975 for a complete list of prohibited transactions.) Examples of disqualified persons are the IRA holder and his or her spouse; the IRA holder's lineal descendants, ascendants, and their spouses; investment advisers and managers; any corporation, partnership, trust, or estate in which the IRA holder has a 50% or greater interest; and anyone providing services to the IRA, such as the trustee or custodian.

Some common questions revolve around the use of real estate and disqualified persons. For instance, you cannot buy a rental property with your IRA and then allow your child to live in it, even if it's rent-free. Similarly, you cannot use it for vacation purposes or let certain family members use it.

You cannot use your IRA for the following purchases or transactions:

→ Borrow money from the IRA for your own use

→ Sell, exchange, or lease property you already own to your IRA

→ Transfer IRA income or assets to disqualified persons

→ Lend IRA money or extend IRA credit to disqualified persons

→ Furnish goods, services, or facilities to disqualified persons

→ Allow fiduciaries to obtain or use the IRA's income or assets for their own interest

There are 3 steps to purchasing investments in a self-directed IRA"

→ Open a self-directed account with someone who handles self-directed IRA accounts for others. This step happens just once, and then, you can contribute money yearly and fund transactions from the account. I have been using the same place in South Florida for about 10 years. They were originally part of the Entrust Group and then branched off and changed names, but I have found them to be very helpful. They have specific forms you must use to deposit money or request money or to purchase or sell a property, and they actually help you every step of the way to be sure you stay in compliance with IRA guidelines. They monitor the transactions and are very helpful when you have questions about anything. The only thing you do is pick what you want to invest in such as a house, gold, mortgages, stocks, etc.

→ Fund your account. You can fund your account by making a contribution or by rolling over funds from another IRA or 401(k) account. Once you fund this account, you do not necessarily need to close the other account you have; you may want to keep some liquid money available in a brokerage or mutual fund account. Many people do not realize you can have more than one IRA, and you do not have to choose to self-direct all of your retirement funds. Do what feels comfortable, as you can always transfer money between your self-directed account and a brokerage account. What you must do is keep Roth IRA funds separate from traditional IRA and 401K money because of the different tax treatment when you do get ready to pull the money out.

→ Choose an investment. If you have an investment in mind, contact your IRA to get started with the necessary paperwork.

With my IRA, I first bought a fixer-upper and paid cash for the property and the rehab, then sold it and returned the money to my account along with all the profit from the transaction. I used a company called Entrust at the time, so the transaction looked like this. I opened my account with Entrust and had them request the funds from Edward Jones. Once the funds were available, I found a property and put it under contract, the contract listing the buyer as Entrust IRA Trust FBO Pamela Keen IRA Account number ######. I wrote the contract, initialed it, and then sent it to the IRA administrator for their signature and requested proof of funds to give the seller's agent, as well as an escrow deposit check for $1,000 which was required by the seller before they would consider my offer. Then I submitted the offer, and once accepted, I had to do a Purchase Authorization Letter (see example in Appendix C) to direct the funds from my account to be wired to the closing agent. Please note, different companies call this by other names such as a Direction Letter. When the closing package was ready, I reviewed it, initialed every page to show my approval, then the actual closing papers were signed by my IRA administrator and the title was vested in Entrust IRA Trust FBO Pamela Keen IRA Account ######, and funds were wired by Entrust from my account. When I needed money for the rehab, I just submitted the bills from the painter, the flooring, etc. to them, and they cut the checks as work was done. Then I sold the home to an end buyer who ended up requesting a new roof, which had not been done previously. The roof then was paid for at the closing and it was shown on the HUD as repairs. I approved the closing statement and initialed all the papers for Entrust. My IRA administrator signed the closing papers and accepted the check for the closing proceeds minus what closing costs I had to pay and the new roof. I was ready to do that again!

What makes my IRA even better is, back when I made less money and started a Roth IRA, I had an old, traditional IRA but I decided to go ahead and pay the taxes on that and convert it all to a Roth when the government gave us a chance to do so. I had to pay the taxes over a two-year period. However, now that all the money I earn in that account is actually tax-free, I am growing the money tax-free and will take it out tax-free. It really does not get better than that. Since this first transaction, I have done a couple more flips; then I bought a house and rented it for two years and finally sold it to the tenant at a nice profit. I bought another house and renovated it, and instead of renting it, I did an installment sale. I made a profit of $25,000 on the flip, took a large down payment with a five-year balloon mortgage at 7% interest, and all the payments are currently going back into my retirement account.

Sometimes I like seller financing better than renting because I don't have any unknown expenses and I know exactly how much I am earning in my account monthly. I have increased my account value from about $75,000, in 2008, to over $250,000 today; and I currently have a stable income coming in from the seller financing and no expenses going out. Were it still a traditional IRA, I would have some tax consequences when I started to pull money out for retirement; so I really am glad I paid the taxes and it can continue to grow tax-free!

IRA Comparisons

Traditional IRA	Roth IRA
Contributions are tax deductible if you do not have access to another plan through your employer Investments grow tax deferred You can't make regular contributions to a traditional IRA after you reach seventy & a half	Contributions are not tax deductible Investments grow tax deferred You can still contribute to a Roth IRA and make rollover contributions to a Roth or traditional IRA regardless of your age

One disadvantage of any IRA account is the limitation on the amount of money you can set aside yearly for retirement. In 2016, the limit was $5,500 ($6,500 if you're age 50 or older), or your taxable compensation for the year if your compensation was less than this dollar limit. There is also a limit on how much you can contribute to a Roth IRA based on your income. If you happen to be self-employed, there are a few other plans that I would consider that can allow you to set aside considerably more money to invest for retirement. Two I am familiar with are the self-directed solo 401K plan, which, in tax year 2016, allows you to set aside up to $18,000; and the second is the defined benefit pension plan, which ca be structured several ways, and it allows even higher contributions for high-income earners, but it comes with a specific set of rules. If you have a larger amount of money to invest, you may want to seek advice and use one of these plans. There are a few things I learned from having my own self-directed retirement plan. One is you can't touch the money, so if you have renters, you must use a property management company. A property manager will collect your rents, pay your bills like taxes and insurance, and send the funds to the IRA monthly less any expenses. Another is that it is difficult to find a lender who will finance for you. There are a few companies that will, but they typically require 30% or more down because the loan must be a non-recourse loan; that means they can only look to the property as collateral, not you.

Chapter 6 Summary

→ There are several tax-advantaged strategies you can use for the purchase and sale of Real Estate for investment.

→ You can sell your personal residence once every two years and there will be no tax on the gain, up to $500,000.

→ You can do a 1031 Exchange and defer the gain to a future date, which gives you more cash to reinvest.

→ You can buy real estate inside a retirement plan such as a traditional IRA, Roth IRA, SEP, 401K or Defined Benefit Plan that is self-directed.

Chapter 7
Federal, State, and Local Laws
That Affect Landlords

I would like to stress that there are going to be many laws that apply to the management of your rentals. There are really three types of laws that you need to be aware of,—federal, state and local—and they vary by state and locality. This chapter may not be the most interesting chapter in the book, but it is very necessary you are aware of everything in it if you plan to own rental property.

Let's start with federal laws that affect landlords. The first of these are Fair Housing Laws. These laws can be found online at www.Hud.gov and are condensed in the table below.

Condensed Fair Housing Laws

Title VIII of the Civil Rights Act of 1968 (Fair Housing Act)

Title VIII as amended, prohibits discrimination in the sale, rental, and financing of dwellings, and in other housing-related transactions, based on race, color, national origin, religion, sex, familial status (including children under the age of 18 living with parents or legal custodians, pregnant women, and people securing custody of children under the age of 18), and disability.

Title VI of the Civil Rights Act of 1964

Title VI prohibits discrimination on the basis of race, color, or national origin in programs and activities receiving federal financial assistance.

Section 504 of the Rehabilitation Act of 1973

Section 504 prohibits discrimination based on disability in any program or activity receiving federal financial assistance.

Section 109 of Title I of the Housing and Community Development Act of 1974

Section 109 prohibits discrimination on the basis of race, color, national origin, sex or religion in programs and activities receiving financial assistance from HUD's Community Development and Block Grant Program.

Title II of the Americans with Disabilities Act of 1990

Title II prohibits discrimination based on disability in programs, services, and activities provided or made available by public entities. HUD enforces Title II when it relates to state and local public housing, housing assistance and housing referrals.

Architectural Barriers Act of 1968

The Architectural Barriers Act requires that buildings and facilities designed, constructed, altered, or leased with certain federal funds after September 1969 must be accessible to and useable by handicapped persons.

Age Discrimination Act of 1975

The Age Discrimination Act prohibits discrimination on the basis of age in programs or activities receiving federal financial assistance.

Title IX of the Education Amendments Act of 1972

Title IX prohibits discrimination on the basis of sex in education programs or activities that receive federal financial assistance.

Note that the Americans with Disabilities Act and Fair Housing have specific requirements dealing with service animals, also called assistance animals or emotional support animals. These types of animals must be allowed if the prospective tenant provides you with proper documentation for the animal. They are not to be considered pets and you are not allowed to charge a nonrefundable pet fee or pet rent to someone with such an animal.

Next, there are laws that apply to homes built before 1978, these are Federal laws that are enforced by the EPA (Environmental Protection Agency). Landlords must give prospective tenants of buildings built before 1978:

→ An EPA-approved information pamphlet on identifying and controlling lead-based paint hazards, Protect Your Family From Lead In Your Home (PDF). This can be downloaded from https://www.epa.gov/lead/real-estate-disclosure

→ Any known information concerning lead-based paint or lead-based paint hazards pertaining to the building. For multi-unit buildings, this requirement includes records and reports concerning common areas and other units when such information was obtained as a result of a building-wide evaluation.

➡ A lead disclosure attachment to the lease, or language inserted in the lease, that includes a "Lead Warning Statement" and confirms that you have complied with all notification requirements. See Appendix F

Another section of the Lead Paint Law deals with renovating homes built before 1978 that could have lead paint. Many people are not aware that:

If the home was built before 1978, the landlord must use an EPA Lead-Certified contractor to work on a home if more than 6 square feet of paint is being disturbed. The latest disclosures for rental and sale of property and rules for contractors, as well as how to get certified and other useful information about lead, can be found by visiting the website https://www.epa.gov/lead

To show just how important these federal laws are, in 2014, a major retailer paid a record $500,000 civil penalty to settle allegations that contractors it hired for home projects violated the federal Lead Renovation, Repair, and Painting (RRP) Rule, the Justice Department and Environmental Protection Agency (EPA). The penalty—by far the largest ever imposed for an RRP violation—stems from investigations at 13 of the retailer's 1,700 stores nationwide, where EPA reviewed records from projects performed by companies working under contract to that retailer. The government complaint was specific to the failure of the retailer to provide proper documentation that the contractors had been properly trained in lead-safe work practices and the use of EPA-approved lead test kits. In addition, there were three homes that were not properly contained and cleaned during the renovations.

> **The EPA is not fooling around. The most recent laws dealing with contractors went into effect in 2010, and many people are not aware of the stiff penalties, so you must follow both the disclosure laws with your tenants and make sure the contractors you hire are certified, or you, too, could pay thousands of dollars in fines.**

Although the above federal laws are very important and must be followed, each state has a specific set of laws called "Landlord Tenant Laws." If you want to browse through the Florida landlord-tenant law, you can find state statutes at Fla. Stat. Ann. §§ 83.40 to 83.682. For any other state, you should be able to find them online or possibly get a copy from your local courthouse landlord tenant section. It is almost certain that there will be separate sections in your state statutes that apply to multifamily, mobile home, and commercial rentals. Pay particular attention to the parts that relate to what maintenance you are required to provide. In Florida, for instance, you must have window screens, but you do not have to provide pest control or trash collection unless you have more than 4 units in a building.

Other important sections in the law will be those on evictions, what rules you must follow holding security deposits, what to do if you want to place a claim for damages against your tenant's security deposit, and laws about abandoned property left on the premises.

There are also separate laws, and possibly tax payments, that apply to short-term rentals. In Florida, tax payments on rentals are handled by the Department of Revenue. Many rentals along the miles and miles of waterfront in Florida are rented for vacation rentals on a short-term basis, and short-term rentals, as well as commercial rentals, in Florida, are taxed.

There are sections of the building code that apply to rented property; things like requirements for smoke detectors, fire extinguishers, water, septic systems, and other local ordinances may apply to rented property.

Other local laws, such as zoning ordinances, determine what you can do with a particular property. A house zoned for single-family residential may not be used to house a business. Land may not be able to be subdivided, and a home may not be able to be converted into a duplex. Check with your city or county. Some counties may require a landlord to obtain a business license for each property. Apartment complexes definitely require licensing and are subject to different requirements than single family homes.

In the case offederal, state and local laws, ignorance is not bliss; ignorance can get you steep fines and/or expensive lawsuits. You are in business, and not knowing is not an excuse for breaking the law.

This section contains a lot of information for those who want to do the management themselves, but you will still have a lot of research and learning to go through gathering the correct info that is applicable to the property you own; and if you own properties in more than one state look for there to be differences. Although federal laws apply to everyone, each state and locality has their own laws that must be followed. Possibly, you will become someone who realizes that the small amount of money you spend monthly to pay a professional to manage the property could actually save you time, money, and aggravation.

Summary

When conducting business as a landlord, you must comply with applicable federal, state and local laws. Federal laws deal with things like antidiscrimination, people with disabilities, and lead paint disclosures. Landlord/tenant laws vary by state and also are different for landlords that deal in single-family homes than those that own apartment complexes or commercial buildings. Local laws have to do with zoning, property use, and things like building permits and health and safety violations. Not knowing the law can land you in court and /or result in fines. Professional property managers are educated and have specialized knowledge in these areas.

Chapter 8

Property Management Basics

There is a lot you need to learn about to be an effective manager, but finding good tenants who stay and take very good care of your property is one of the very important functions that needs to be covered. In order to find good tenants, you must first determine what it is that good tenants want in a rental property. Below are several things that I believe are very important to most "good" tenants:

→ Safe neighborhood

→ House that is clean and in good repair with a nice functional kitchen and good appliances, including a refrigerator

→ Fair rent for the current market and reasonable rate increases at renewals

→ Privacy

→ A house that is not for sale

→ Located in good public school district

Washers and dryers and other furnishings are not really important. In fact, those things are more likely to attract shorter-term tenants. Good tenants who plan to stay in your home have their own furniture already. There is no magic here. If you already own some houses, do they meet these criteria? If not, is there something you can do to make the house more desirable? If the only answer is to pick it up and put it somewhere else, I recommend trying to sell and get something in a better location. If selling is not an option and your home is in an area of high crime and/or subpar schools, you may find that you have to leave it vacant longer and turn down several prospective tenants before finding one that meets all of your criteria. It will be better in the long run to wait for the right tenant than to evict them later for not paying rent or for destruction of property.

Always get the house in good condition and have it professionally cleaned before you rent it. If you advertise a dirty house that needs repairs, you may attract a dirty tenant or someone who has been turned down for other residences because of credit or other issues. Tenants often promise to do work or clean it themselves, but they rarely do. If they are not happy about the condition of the home when they move in, you will hear about it again and again, and they will be less likely to leave the home in good condition when they leave. Don't neglect cleaning windows, inside of cabinets and drawers, under the sink, etc. I recommend finding a professional cleaning service that is used to cleaning rentals—they are worth the cost. I would like to talk a little more about property selection, even though we did talk about it in a previous chapter.

This chapter is going to relate your selection specifically to what kind of property will be most appealing to good tenants. I think now that we are talking about what tenants want is a good time to go over some more specifics that were not covered earlier and give some examples from my management experience of why these things are so important.

Let's talk about neighbors. When you are selecting a property that you intend to rent out for a long term investment, buy in mostly owner occupied neighborhoods, and pay attention to the homes on either side and across the street from the home you are considering. Ask yourself, do the yards and exteriors look well-kept and show that the occupants care about the exterior appearance? Are there loud, barking, scary dogs next door? Does the yard look like it houses its own junkyard or have broken down cars and boats parked in the yard or on the driveway? In my experience, if you have bad neighbors, it will most likely directly affect the quality of tenant you can attract to live in the home. If the house you are considering is the one that looks bad on the exterior, I suggest you spend wisely for things like pressure washing, painting, and low maintenance landscaping and then expect your tenants to maintain it during their tenancy.

Another piece of advice is to avoid unique houses with strange or outdated floorplans, as they tend to appeal to less people. A yard that is fenced or can be easily fenced is also a plus. Most tenants that rent single family homes have kids, pets or both, so they often are specifically looking for a house with a fenced yard. Homes with only 1 bathroom can be more difficult to rent, and homes with too much acreage may be problematic to get the tenant to take care of the grounds.

There are going to be 4 things every landlord wishes for all his tenants. They are the following:

➜ The tenant pays on time.

➜ The tenant stays forever.

➜ The tenant never calls to complain.

➜ The tenant takes care of the home, makes minor repairs, and does routine maintenance, such as fixes the toilet flapper, changes the air conditioner filter regularly, fertilizes the grass, and trims the shrubs.

So you have purchased what you believe will be a good rental property in a good, safe neighborhood with above-average schools, but it was a foreclosure and it needs a little "love" before you will be able to rent it to a good tenant. My advice to you is that you don't try to cut too many corners fixing the property, and if you intend to hire a property manager or management company perhaps you might call and ask them to walk through the home with you and see if they have any recommendations if there are things you are unsure of.

In general, I suggest getting rid of loud colors—paint neutral colors with bright white trim; get rid of outdated wallpaper and paneling; make sure the appliances are good, matching, and clean; make sure the flooring is in good condition—if not, replace it. Install inexpensive blinds on all the windows, have the house professionally cleaned, pressure wash the exterior if needed, and have the shrubs trimmed and grass mowed. Families with pets and/or children prefer a fenced yard, so if the yard is not fenced or is only partially fenced consider fencing it in.

As a property manager, one of my jobs is to try and pick good owners and send not-so-good owners elsewhere to do business. Owners who do not listen to our suggestions upfront often find later that they should have. For the past couple of years, my company has rented between 400-500 homes a year, which represents about 10-11% of the homes that rented in the Pensacola MLS in the past year, so we do pay attention to what rents fast and what does not. Often, there are just some minor tweaks that can be done to make the home more desirable. Attention to detail is so important! I hope this does not offend anyone, but I have found that some men are definitely not as picky as us ladies are, so when you are working on a home getting it ready, I highly recommend having a woman look at the home to double-check it. After all, it's a fact that there will, most likely, be a woman helping to make the decision on what house to rent; so it pays to get someone of the opposite sex to look at the property and make recommendations.

So you have a home that is rent-ready. Now what?

The next things you need to do once you get the property rent ready are to set the rent and deposit and begin to market the home. Setting the rent used to be more difficult for the novice, but with information readily available on sites like Zillow®, you can go look at their rent or sales values, Zestimates®, for any address. Keep in mind, however, that this is merely the result of a computer-generated model and that rents in different neighborhoods can vary quite a bit. Rent will also vary with the condition and amenities of the home. Homes that have an outdated kitchen, older appliances, only 1 bathroom, or odd floorplans, i.e. you have to walk through one bedroom to get to another one, will rent but not at the same price as something that is bigger and more updated.

Now is a good time to call a local property manager and have a conversation with them. You may find you can get more rent if you use a manager than you can when you rent it yourself.

If you still want to go it alone, the next step will be to start marketing the home. This may also require some research and trial and error to see what works best in your area, but I will suggest some things that have worked well for me.

Place a nice "For Rent" sign at the property if there are no restrictions against signs in the area. Make sure the phone number is clearly legible when people drive by. The sign will not only get you calls but it will help identify the property easily if people have seen the home advertised on the Internet and are doing a drive-by. One thing I have learned from experience is always suggest when you are talking to prospective renters that they do a drive-by. This will save you from showing up to an appointment to find you have been stood up. If they don't like the outside or the neighborhood, they are not likely to stick around. Prospects now can actually go online and "drive by" the property using something like Google Earth, but my point is that they should be familiar with the surrounding neighborhood and know this is an area they want to live before you set an appointment to show them the property.

Over 91 % of renters and buyers are going to be looking online, so you need to take some good photos of the property and find some good online sites to advertise your property. Craigslist® and Zillow® are two good places to start. You can find these places by going to https://www.zillow.com/rental-manager/posts/all/ and http://craigslist.org. Be sure to post interior and exterior pictures of the property as well as pictures of any neighborhood parks or other amenities you want to feature. If you own property in an area near a military base there is a great site called http://AHRN.com (Automated Housing Referral Network®

Evaluate the activity you are getting from your sign and online advertising. You may want to place an ad in an inexpensive local publication, especially if you want to target seniors as they are least likely to be looking online. If you are advertising and getting calls to request info but not showing requests you need to reevaluate the price. If the price is too high for the market and the neighborhood no one will want to view it because they are finding something similar for less money. If you are getting calls and showings and people are walking away and not renting you need to ask for feedback. Don't take it personally. There are reasons why people are not renting your house. If it is something about the property that can be fixed, then by all means try to fix it! If there is something you cannot fix or it would cost too much to fix, you have to compensate by making it a better price or by offering an incentive such as a lower deposit or move-in special of some kind.

There are a few other factors that should be considered. Depending on where your property is located, there may be seasonal differences in the amount of rent you can get, unless you want to accept longer vacancies. As a general rule, more people move in the summer for a number of reasons. One reason is families with children in school prefer to move when school is not in session. Moving also sometimes requires children to switch schools because of local school districts. College towns definitely also have a specific timing preference, coinciding with the beginning of the fall semester. In Pensacola, Florida, we definitely have more people moving in the summer, and the worst time of year to be experiencing a vacancy is November and December: people do not like to move over the holidays!! Keep in mind an empty house costs the landlord money for every day it stays vacant, especially when you have a mortgage payment to make and possibly utilities! Vacant homes are also more likely to be broken into and vandalized. Most insurance companies will consider cancelling your policy or denying a claim if they find the property has been vacant more than 30 days. If your property is vacant, you must keep the yard maintained and keep utility services established to prevent the appearance that it is obviously vacant.

Keeping good tenants in place is very important for investments to perform well over time. Anticipating vacancies and staying on top of maintenance and repairs, as well as having relationships with handy men and cleaning people, will help you attract and keep good quality tenants.

Chapter 8 Summary

Prepping your home for renting keeping in mind what good tenants want in a home, setting the right rent rate and deposit for the area, researching and knowing your target market and having a good marketing plan, evaluating your marketing results, and aiming to keep vacancy between tenants at a minimum will result in you being a happy landlord with happy tenants and producing the best possible return on your investment.

Chapter 9

Dealing with Tenants

My company is a large management company and to be sure we are in compliance with all local, state and federal laws, we have established tenant selection criteria. We use these criteria to approve or deny applicants for our rental properties. The first thing we do is have our tenants review our tenant criteria and fill out a written application. See Appendix D. I suggest if you are going to manage the property yourself you should require the same. They must agree to a full background check for which we charge them the fee. Before they pay the fee, we let the applicant know upfront what our requirements are. Some of the things we use are credit score, judgements, evictions, criminal convictions, employment, and past landlord references as well as verification of the amount of their current income. We require the applicant must have documented income of at least three times the rent. They must provide us with current verification from their paystubs if W2- employed, and we do require self-employed individuals to either submit several months' bank statements showing the deposits or their most recent tax return.

I have found that tenants who are unable to prove their income often turn out to be chronic late payers or, worse may need to be evicted for nonpayment when they get behind. We do not compromise on this. Retirees should be able to show their income, even if it comes from several sources such as social security or income from a 401K or other brokerage account. Again, a tax return may be needed to pull it all together and make sure they can afford the rent. The only time income is not a factor is if you are dealing with Section 8 housing where the rent payment is guaranteed by a government agency.

If you have someone that is moving from another area and has not secured employment I would not advise using past income as verification if it's going to stop when they move. If you are fairly confident the person is a professional and will obtain employment that will meet the criteria, you might consider having them pay several months' rent in advance. In the case of college students or other younger renters that may not meet all the criteria you may want to consider using a guarantor or cosigner, such as a parent, and use their income and credit to meet the criteria. In situations like this, because we are managing for other people, we would always get the property owners' written permission to use a cosigner or to consider a tenant that varies from our normal criteria. For tenants with good income and references, but a marginal credit score, you might consider accepting them if they are willing to pay a higher security deposit. If you are self-managing make sure you document everything, especially if you have more than one applicant for a particular property. Just make sure the criteria you are using is objective and measurable and not related to anything that could be viewed by others as discriminatory. Remember, violations of Federal Fair Housing Laws can result in fines as high as $11,000 per offense!

If you turn down an applicant for one of your properties or if you agree to rent but require them to pay a higher deposit than what was advertised, per fair credit guidelines you must give them a written turn down letter. See Appendix E. Legitimate reasons you can use are the following:

→ Insufficient income or inability to verify income

→ Lack of rental history or poor past landlord reference

→ Sex offender

→ Past eviction

→ Lack of steady employment

You cannot turn someone down for having children, being too old, or having a service animal.

Once you accept an applicant, you should notify them and get them to put up a deposit and sign the lease as soon as possible. We require them to pay this in certified funds. I learned that lesson years ago. The last thing you want is a tenant who has just moved in to your home when you find out their check for both the security deposit and the rent bounced!

You will get tenants who want to pay some of the money now and the rest next week when they get paid. My advice is don't do it.

If you have a property that is part of a condominium or homeowners' association, make sure the lease references the association and have the tenant acknowledge in writing that you are giving them a copy of the covenants and/or the rules and regulations and they agree to abide by them. If the tenant fails to comply with the rules and regulations you the homeowner are the one who will be given a fine for the violation, and it is your responsibility to deal with correcting the issue or getting your tenant to do so.

Be sure to document with receipts and photos any work you had done to the property just prior to renting it, as well as do what I call a move-in inspection with the tenant where they sign off on the property condition as of the time of occupancy. There are times when, despite your best efforts the cleaning lady misses a few things or the dishwasher won't drain. You want to address any move in issues quickly so you will have happy tenants.

Know what is required of landlords in your particular state, as laws vary. Sometimes you will get requests from tenants for things that are either very picky cosmetic issues or that are not required maintenance. You are not required by law to fix everything. In each case, you have to determine if the request is reasonable or not and what the law says. It is usually best to try and please your tenant; however, your tenants need to realize that each home may have some things the landlord is not willing to do. Here in Florida, a landlord is required to provide window screens but is not required to provide pest control unless there are more than 4 units; however, if a tenant moves in to one of my rentals with an initial complaint of roaches or fleas, I will generally agree to provide them with a one-time service and inform them that they can continue the service at their expense.

You will find over time that not every tenant will be a good one. When you get good ones, it would be wise to treat them well, take care of any maintenance issues that come up in a timely manner, and show them your appreciation. It will be in your best interest to get good tenants to stay and renew their lease. As previously discussed, every day of vacancy costs the landlord money, so consider offering them a small incentive such as a professional carpet cleaning or a new ceiling fan or a gift card when they renew their lease and make sure any rent increases are reasonable and in line with market rates.

One thing you must do is inspect your property, inside and out, on a regular basis. Tenants who are not taking good care of the home may pay their rent on time and not call in maintenance requests, but you need to see the inside of the home to be sure they are not damaging it. I recommend an inspection after they have been living there for about 90 days and about every 3-4 months thereafter. If the first inspection is good, you may be able to forego additional inspections till a few months before their lease is to be renewed. Always inspect the home at least annually before agreeing to renew the lease. If there is damage that was caused by the tenants or they are not keeping up with the yard and landscaping, you may want to give them a notice with an opportunity to cure the defect. One thing you must understand about tenants is that not everyone lives by the same standards. Look for damages or excessive wear and tear, not dirty dishes in the sink or kid's toys laying around the house. Ultimately, it is your property and you may choose whether or not to renew their lease agreement, so if you are unhappy with the way they are caring or not caring for your property, you can ask them to leave at the end of their lease.

The story you are about to read is true, and I use it to instill in you the importance of regular inspections. This tenant had been living in this property for 5 1/2 years and always paid the rent on time with a few exceptions, and never called in to request maintenance issues. Although this is not the typical tenant, this is one that landlords fear, and a story like this can keep someone from wanting to own rental property at all. The property described in the story below is not in the best location, and the rent was on the lower end for a three-bedroom house. This is one of the reasons I stress buying homes in the best location you can find as you will attract better quality tenants.

"No amount of binge-watching Hoarders could have prepared me. I had been working as a rental inspector barely a month and was still learning. I was told that the tenant I had been assigned to do the annual inspection had been there for five years, and they had never been able enter this home to do a full inspection.

The tenant would reschedule, always leave her dog, a Chow mix, out to guard the home, or, in one case, change the locks so we couldn't get in. My assignment was to try to do a full inspection and get photos of the interior of the home. I was told the tenant had been aware we needed to inspect that day for about two weeks and had already rescheduled once, but she still had called to try and reschedule again, so I was not sure if I would be able to complete the inspection or not, but I had a key to the home.

I arrived at the home and knocked on the door. No answer. I decided to take some exterior photos while waiting for the tenant to arrive. The yard was extremely overgrown, with weeds and some grass growing over knee-high. Large unkempt bushes had grown so high on the left side of the home that they were resting on the roof of the house. As I was taking pictures of a window AC unit my eye caught something flying around the window. As I looked closer, I realized there were at least twenty live flies flying around on the inside of one window. This was the case for almost every other window on the front of the house.

It was now past the scheduled time for the tenant to meet me, but they had not arrived, and I was beginning to feel like they probably would not show up. I also noticed a strange odor emitting from the unopened front door, along with dog hair on the outside stoop. I texted my supervisor asking if there was another inspector near me to offer some backup.

Unfortunately, there wasn't, so I decided to attempt entry. I knocked again, still no answer. I took the key, unlocked the deadbolt, and then the main lock. As I slowly opened the door, I tried to yell, "Anybody home?" but the smell hit me so hard, I couldn't finish saying "home." I had never smelled anything like this before. It was literally indescribable. I stepped back to gather myself and then continued to swing the door open.

I stood at the stoop with the door wide open, staring at something I had only seen on reality shows and horror films: piles of stuff, junk, and trash stacked so high you couldn't walk over it. There were two paths you could take, one to the left, the other to the right. I stepped inside and was startled by a lady standing in the corner. I was about to say hello when I realized it was just a giant statue of Mary with one arm broken off. I started to take a few pictures to document what I was seeing: large piles of dog hair, black plastic bags of garbage stacked on top of each other, empty garbage bags lining the floors, and a huge spider web and its maker in a fake plant right next to the front door. I started to move forward and continue to take photos, but was stopped in my tracks when I saw it: the body of a dog, the Chow that had guarded this home and kept us from inspecting this house had been there all this time, lying motionless on the floor. For some stupid reason, I called out, "doggie?" but the dog didn't move, nor had he moved after I knocked on the door and called out. The dog looked dead.

I took a picture of the dog from the front door, backed out of the house and closed the door while texting my supervisor that there was a dead dog on the floor and a very bad smell coming from the home. Fearing for the safety of the tenant, she called the police to have them search the home room by room. I was then told to hang tight, that the officers were on the way.

A few minutes later, two police SUVs pulled up, along with an ambulance. I explained the situation and what I had seen. They decided to go in. I waited by the edge of the yard, next to the mailbox. The officers knocked loudly, spoke loudly, and entered the home. I'll never forget that horrible smell emitting from the home. One of the two EMTs standing near me said, "That smells like a dead body." A couple of seconds later, I heard one of the officer's yell, "DOG!" followed by loud barking and two officers exiting the house. They said that the first officer had stepped over the dog to enter the hallway, but as the second officer stepped near it, the dog came to life and started snapping and barking at the officers. No guns or tasers were needed, though. One of the officers quickly sprayed pepper spray in the direction of the Chow, giving them time to exit. They decided to call in animal control, so they could remove the animal from the home and conclude their search.

Animal control arrived while the officers were gearing up to search the house. This time, they decided to put on air respirators and special covers for their boots. They went in, and soon the animal control agent walked out with the dog collared. The dog could barely walk and had left the majority of its hair in mats in the home. I was overcome with sadness — not because there was a human being actually living in the conditions, but that this animal had been subjected to the living conditions that animal control felt weren't suitable for a dog and, therefore, took it away to what I know were better living conditions.

The officers re-entered the home, finished their room-to-room inspection and, thankfully, found no dead bodies. One of the officers, once out, removing his respirator, said he couldn't believe someone was actually living inside this home and that it should be condemned."
—Rick Pluckett

I'm sure you now would like to know what happened after that? A seven-day notice without cure was posted on the tenant's door, giving her seven days to vacate the premises. Of course, she did not move, and an eviction was then filed. She still did not move; she actually hired an attorney and contested the eviction. The attorney stated the house was in disarray because she had a medical condition and that she should have been given an opportunity to correct the deficiencies. He also stated that the deficiencies had since been corrected and brought signed affidavits for the judge. In our county, they request that cases like this go before a mediator first, and the judge sent the parties to meet with the mediator. The owner worried that the eviction was going to be overturned because the attorney made the tenant look like a saint, and technically, he had never even gotten pictures of the entire house that day, only the front room because the police told Rick not to enter. Immediately upon entering the mediation room, the tenant started crying and apologized to the property owner for letting the home get in that condition. The mediator asked what, if anything, could be done to resolve this case before it went before the judge. The tenant agreed to hire a professional cleaning company and an exterminator at her expense, clean up the yard, hire someone to get the shrubs cut back and off the roof and house, and allow my company to come back and inspect the home as soon as that had been arranged. Also, that the tenant would allow quarterly inspections of the home in the future for as long as she lives there. She was informed that, since she was on a month-to-month tenancy, she could be given a 15-day notice to vacate the premises if any of the inspections were found unsatisfactory. Three weeks later, a notice was posted, a re-inspection was done and nothing had changed, so the owner filed an affidavit requesting a writ of possession, which was granted. The cleanup was costly and difficult.

I have been involved with managing my own and other people's rentals since 1978, so I think it's safe to say that I have a lot of expertise in this area. One thing I learned over the years is not everyone is good at property management, and there are a lot of I's to dot and T's to cross on a daily basis, and you must either resolve yourself to get good at the business of property management or put into your business plan enough margin so you can afford to hire a professional manager to do it for you. The job of the professional property manager is to first of all minimize the owner's risk of having this type of thing occur. If a situation like the one above happens in spite of the manager's best screening process, it would be the manager's job to deal with it for the property owner.

In order to be successful at property management you have to be a good people person, but you also have to be organized enough to be able to accomplish many tasks within the same day, and you need to have a team of dependable service professionals that can get the job done when a tenant calls in a maintenance issue. This is one instance where you can't do it all yourself, unless you know plumbing, electrical, air conditioning, appliance repair, painting, carpentry, etc. The following is just a monthly timeline to help you organize and keep things from slipping through the cracks.

Daily - return calls, handle maintenance requests, check email, showings, lease signings; Turnovers and New Properties: advertised, put and on the web, utilities on and repairs/cleanup completed to make ready for new tenants

Weekly - check and follow up on all your pending work orders for status; this will keep things from falling through the cracks and hopefully eliminate the Friday afternoon phone calls when the tenant who called in on Monday with a request for a plumbing or AC repair is upset because no one called or showed up.

1st through 5th - charge, collect and post rents

6th through 7th - Call tenants who have not paid to find out why and when they may be able to pay; prepare and post three-day notices to tenants who have not paid the rent. When delivering notices, do exterior inspection of the property and check for any maintenance needs. Has the yard been kept up by the tenant? Make notes of findings for follow up.

10th through 15th - lease renewal letter must be mailed for leases expiring the following month; ex. March 10th-15th letters for leases ending April 30th

15th through end of the month

Before signing a new lease schedule property inspection.

If there are discrepancies on the inspection a phone call or nice letter needs to be used. 7-day notices may be used for repeat offenders or SERIOUS violations, and leases should not be renewed unless they are corrected.

Establishing the rules with your tenants is something that must be done when they move in. Make it clear in writing what's considered an emergency and what isn't. You should keep tenant relations professional. It may not be a good idea to socialize with your tenants because you are basically the boss, and you need them to take you seriously. At our office, we have a tenant handbook which we give to the tenants at lease signing, and they sign that they understand it is part of their lease. See Appendix G for a copy of the handbook we use at my company.

A successful landlord thinks ahead. You should be prepared for anything Mother Nature could throw your way, based on your location: hurricanes, earthquakes, tornadoes, fires, and floods are examples. Since my company is in Florida, our tenant handbook provides tenants information about hurricane preparedness. We also have a clause in our lease that allows lease termination in the event of damage that makes the property uninhabitable. Think about what disasters could occur in your area, and make a plan for them. A good resource for emergency preparedness information is https://www.ready.gov

Fires may or may not be an act of nature. Regardless of the cause, they can spread quickly. Be sure your property is in compliance with local fire codes and includes fire extinguishers, smoke detectors, and carbon monoxide detectors; and instruct your tenants on how to check them and change the batteries. Smoke detectors have an expiration date. When you go in to do property inspections, be sure to check them and replace them if expired.

Every landlord needs an answer to the question, how long should house components and improvements last? That is a topic we deal with every day in the property management business. The true life of any household material depends on the quality of the installation, the use, climate conditions, and if regular maintenance is performed. I am going to start by giving you some data that was compiled by the National Association of Home Builders that estimates the average life expectancy of many home components and then tell you why this is important and how you should use this information in dealing with tenants.

Gas Ranges - 15 years

Dryers / Refrigerators 13 years

Dishwashers/Microwaves - 9 years

Compactors - 6 years

Countertops Natural Stone - lifetime

Cultured Marble – 20 years

Decks - 15-20 years, depending on climate

Doors: Exterior fiberglass, steel, and wood - will last as
long as house stands

Vinyl doors - 20 years

Screen Doors - 40 years

French Doors - 30-50 years

Faucets/Kitchen Sinks - 50 years

Fixtures: Faucets - 15 years

Shower Doors - 20 years

Showerheads/Toilets - lifetime

Flooring: Wood, marble, slate & granite - 100 years

Linoleum - 25 years

Carpet - 8-10 years

Garage Doors: 10-15 years

Home Technology Security Systems- 5-10 years

Heat and Smoke Detectors - 5-10 years

Heating/Venting/HVAC Systems - 15-20 years

AC Tankless Water Heaters - 20 years

Electric or Gas Water Heaters - 10 years

In my experience, the numbers above are more applicable to owner- occupied dwellings because, in reality, most tenants will not take care of a property as well as an owner does. A rule of thumb is whenever there is a question about who should pay for something the landlord should pay, but there are times when you will feel that something should be deducted as damages from the tenant's security deposit, or you want to get tenants out because they are causing damage to your property. Many tenants are experts at what I call "normal wear and tear." They will dispute the charges and possibly even go to court and claim the damages were merely "normal wear and tear." I am going to suggest some steps you should take to make it easier for you to make the deductions and win.

The first step in determining wear and tear is good record keeping. You need to keep records of when you purchased items and/or when they were installed. You cannot be expected to know how long they will last if you do not know the age. If they were present when you bought the property, try to find out their history from the previous owner. Many times you can get product manuals and other warranty info from a previous owner.

Another really important thing to have is pictures of the home prior to the tenant moving in and a tenant move-in checklist, signed by the tenant. You can either walk through the home with the tenant when they move in and fill out the checklist and have them sign it or give it to them when you give them the keys and give them 2-3 days to fill it out and turn it back in signed. Without this properly filled out, the tenant can always claim the damage was there when he or she moved in.

When a tenant moves in, let them know that you want to be notified as soon as any damage occurs that needs repair. Also, let them know what you expect them to do to maintain the home, such as changing the filter in the inside heater/AC unit once a month and being in charge of routine pest control. We also stress to our tenants that if there is a plumbing leak they are responsible for turning off the water to minimize damage until someone can get there. Stoppages because of hair or grease in a drain or toilets backing up because a child placed a toy in the bowl are things that while they may be an emergency at the time, you can use for examples to educate your tenants and make them responsible for the bills. Failure to change the A/C filter can cause the coils to become coated with dust and/or pet hair which causes the unit not to function as it was designed to and shortens the life span of the equipment. It would be appropriate to charge a tenant for the cleaning of the unit if a property inspector says the filter was dirty.

Evictions, such as the one from the earlier example, are not something you want to have to experience; however, you need to know the process in your particular state. I am not going to go into detail here. Suffice it to say that you can usually get the forms and a packet of information from the local courthouse, where they will most likely have a section especially for landlord/tenant issues. Be sure to carefully consider your state landlord tenant act. Before you file, you need to clearly identify who you're evicting and why. You must identify the illegal roommate as part of the eviction process if you are evicting for that reason. The first step of the process is a notice to quit. This can either be a demand to either pay the rent or move or a demand to stop doing something, such as smoking in a nonsmoking home. The notice should include the names of the occupants, the property address, and the reason for the notice. It should give the tenant details on the amount of time they have to resolve the problem or vacate by a certain date. Once you file, you should not accept any money from the occupants you are trying to remove, as that will stop the process and you will have to start over with your eviction. But if the notice is given for nonpayment of rent you must accept the rent payment if they bring it in during the grace period that is listed on the paperwork, but not after that date. The next step is the summons and complaint, followed by an answer from the tenant that will prompt a court date to be set. The judge will then hear both parties' testimony and rule, hopefully in your favor. You will receive a written order called a writ of possession from the court to remove the tenant from the dwelling and, in most cases, you will be required to meet a police officer at the property to take over possession. In our area, we must either have a key or bring a locksmith to the eviction, and we are required to put the tenants' possessions curbside and change the locks immediately so the old occupants can no longer get in.

When your property stays rented, you are going to be making money; however, there will come a day when your tenant will either give you notice they intend to leave, or you will ask them to leave because either they are not paying the rent in a timely manner, or they are not taking care of your property. When one of those events occurs, you must have a turnover plan. I suggest you implement the turnover plan as soon as you know of a pending vacancy. Don't make the mistake of waiting till the property is actually vacant. I suggest when a tenant gives you notice, you look at your last inspection report and pictures, and if they have been in the property awhile, you should anticipate there will be items that need to be repaired or upgraded as well as expect there to be some painting and cleaning. A good plan would include making an appointment with your tenant to walk through the property and identify these things, as well as get measurements of the rooms so you can get flooring estimates, and of all the windows because most likely you will need to replace a few blinds. Pay attention to kitchen appliances, lighting, ceiling fans, that may be outdated or worn and need replacing. Make a plan and get things lined up to begin anything needed the day after the tenant moves.

When the tenant gives notice is also the time to begin marketing for a new tenant. First you should reevaluate the rental rates and see if it makes sense to go up on the rent. Follow the same steps you took to market your property the first time, and be sure to update any websites or Internet property listings you may have to reflect current information. If you know your tenant will turn in keys the last day of the month, give yourself at least 5-7 business days to turn the property around. We send our tenants a set of move-out guidelines when they give notice and even give them names of cleaning and carpet cleaning people they can call that are on our approved vendor list; however, not all of our homes get turned back to us move-in ready. Keep in mind that even if tenants do clean the home, there may be maintenance items that need attention that are not their responsibility, and it is best to get these all done before the new tenant moves in.

I have tried to give you the basics of property management in the last few chapters, but I would like to discuss the reasons you may want to consider hiring a property manager and how you can go about finding a good one.

As you progress as a real estate investor, you may find that the extra work involved with managing properties and tenants takes more time than you have available in the day, especially if you also still have another career or job. Good property management includes everything from marketing to leasing to qualified tenants, keeping them happy and dealing with maintenance and repairs, as well as other tenant issues. So the first reason you may want to consider hiring is a manager so you will have more time to spend with your family. Another reason to have a property manager is that they lease properties for lots of other people like yourself; they have a knowledge database that is current. They know what rent a house will bring, and they know what specific property upgrades can get you higher rent.

The third main reason you may want to consider professional management is the law. If you watch the news, you will notice that state and federal laws that affect you as a landlord are frequently being revised. It is often difficult to keep up. Good property managers usually will belong to associations that subscribe to legislature monitoring systems which enables them to learn about new laws being passed.

The fourth reason you should consider hiring a property manager is they should have a web presence where they advertise properties and have connections with potential tenants. They also should have well defined tenant selection criteria and good screening methods designed to keep the bad tenants out and protect you from renting to the wrong tenant.

What services will a manager provide? In general, they will advertise for tenants, show the property, screen applicants, prepare leases, collect rents, hold security deposits, arrange for maintenance and repairs, handle emergencies, enforce the lease, accounting, property turnover, evictions, and security deposit disputes. Since they will be handling money that comes from your tenants and goes to you, find out how they will collect rent and when they will disperse your money to you. Other questions are what kind of accounting do they use and what do the monthly statements look like, do they have online access to statements for owners?

Before you hire a manager, you should ask the following questions:

→ How long have you had a real estate license and how long have you been a property manager?

→ What are your fees?

→ Do you mark up the maintenance, if so, how much?

→ What professional organizations do you belong to and do you have any professional designations?

→ How does your management program work?

Before you hire a property manager, do some due diligence. You should not use the fact that one manager charges less as a sole reason to hire them. Make sure you are getting apples for apples, and find out exactly what you are getting for the money you will be paying. You should check their credentials: ask for references and check them out to see if they belong to the local Chamber of Commerce and the Better Business Bureau and if they are in good standing. Many great property managers are out there, but don't assume anyone with a real estate license is qualified to manage your property. Your real estate agent should be able to help you with data before you purchase to determine the potential rent that you can get by finding comparable homes for rent and that have rented on the local multiple listing service which they have access to. They may even be able to advertise and help you find a tenant if that is your biggest concern, but that is only part of the equation. So opt for someone with a proven track record who has been in the business for a while. Two good professional associations that good managers may be a part of a r e the National Association of Residential Property Managers® (NARPM®) and Institute of Real Estate Management (IREM). I am a member of NARPM®. If you own single-family homes and are looking for management I recommend you go to www.narpm.org . They have a property manager locator on the site.

Chapter 9 Summary

→ **Stick with established criteria and use a written application when selecting tenants; don't forego the background check.**

→ **If you turn someone down, use fair credit guidelines and you must give them a turndown letter in writing.**

→ **Document with photos or video the property condition before the tenant moves in; have them sign off on a written property condition report, and do property inspections during the tenancy. The first one starting about 90 days after they move in then at least every 3- 6 months after that.**

➜ Get organized and keep track of when rents are due if notices were posted. Don't let your tenants get too far behind on the rent, and do not forget to keep up with property maintenance. Establish a good team of maintenance providers for the things you cannot do yourself, such as electrical and heating and air.

➜ Establish rules with your tenants; keep the relationship professional.

➜ Have an emergency plan.

➜ Consider hiring a property manager if you can't do it all yourself. Find a good one by doing your due diligence.

Conclusion

In this book, I have tried to give you all the basic information you will need to start making sound, low risk, profitable real estate investments. Armed with this book plus some of your own research about the local market and the laws in the state and locality you plan to purchase property, you too can build substantial wealth investing in real estate. I have learned along the way that nothing is 100% certain, so I always have a contingency plan for all of my investment property, and I keep cash reserves for the unexpected. I have personally been involved in transactions using all the techniques found within this book. I have found success and created my wealth by combining short- and long-term investment strategies. Right now, I still buy, hold, and rent single-family homes and duplexes, I buy fixer uppers to rehab and flip, and I owner-finance some of the homes I sell. I currently hold real estate and mortgages in my IRA accounts instead of stocks and bonds like the majority of people. I have quite a nest egg of passive income for my retirement, but I plan to continue to invest and help others to do so because it is my passion.

You too, can find your niche and be successful at building wealth using Real Estate. No matter which area of real estate or other career you choose to pursue, make it your passion and never stop learning. I hope this book will help each and every one of you find success in your personal journey.

Appendix A
Real Estate Broker Requirements for Licensure in the State of Florida

Hold an active real estate sales associate license and complete 24 months (effective 7/1/08) real estate experience during the 5-year period preceding becoming licensed as a broker or a licensed real estate sales associate or broker who has real estate experience in another state may apply the experience toward a Florida real estate broker license if the applicant has held an active sales associate or a valid broker license for at least 24 months during the preceding 5 years. If the applicant is claiming experience from a jurisdiction other than Florida, attach to the application a current certification of real estate license history (not more than 30 days old) from the licensing agency of that jurisdiction. The real estate license must have been obtained from the real estate licensing authority by completing its education and examination requirements. NOTE: If the applicant holds a Florida real estate sales associate license, (s)he must fulfill the sales associate post-licensing education requirement before being eligible to obtain a broker license. This method does not exempt a sales associate who holds a Florida sales associate license from successfully completing the sales associate post-licensing course.

Successfully complete a FREC approved pre-licensing course for brokers consisting of 72 classroom hours and covering the topics required by the FREC. The course is valid for licensure purposes for two years after the course completion date. Applicants with a permanent physical disability, as defined by FREC Rule 61J2-3.013(2), may qualify for a correspondence pre-licensing course if unable, due to a permanent physical disability, to attend the site where the course is conducted.

Submit a completed application, electronic fingerprints, and appropriate fee.

Pass the Florida Real Estate Broker Examination with a grade of at least 75. 5. Submit a completed DBPR RE 13 Broker Transactions form to activate the license, otherwise the license is issued in an inactive status. 6. Successfully complete a FREC-approved post-licensing course for brokers consisting of at least 60 classroom hours prior to the expiration of the initial broker license.

Appendix B
Summary of IRS Guidelines
Pertaining to 1031 Exchanges

Always to trade "across" or up, but never trade down in order to avoid receipt of boot either as cash, debt reduction or both.

Always to bring cash to the closing of the replacement property to cover loan fees or other charges which are not qualified costs.

Do not receive property which is not like-kind.

Do not over-finance the replacement property, since financing should be limited to the amount of money necessary to close on the replacement property in addition to exchange funds which will be brought to the replacement property closing.

The 1031 exchange...

begins on the date the deed records, or the date possession is transferred to the buyer, whichever comes earlier.

and ends on the earlier of the following:

180 days after it begins, or the date the Exchanger's tax return is due, including extensions, for the taxable year in which the relinquished property is transferred.

The identification period is the first 45 days of the exchange period. The exchange period is a maximum of 180 days. If the Exchanger has multiple relinquished properties, the deadlines begin on the transfer date of the first property. These deadlines may not be extended for any reason, except for the declaration of a presidentially declared disaster.

A deadline that falls on any weekend day or holiday does not permit extension. For example, if your tax return is due April 15, but that date falls on a Saturday, then your tax return due date is forwarded to the first business day following April 15, or Monday, April 17. However, if a deadline falls on a Sunday, the requirements for the exchange must be met no later than the last business day prior to the deadline date, i.e. the prior Friday. Failure to comply with these deadlines may result in a failed exchange. IRS rules also control the length of time that the replacement property must be held before it may either be sold or used to enter into a new tax deferred exchange.

In order to qualify for a 1031 exchange, certain rules must be followed:

Both the relinquished property and the replacement property must be held either for investment or for productive use in a trade or business. A personal residence cannot be exchanged.

The asset must be of like-kind. Real property must be exchanged for real property, although a broad definition of real estate applies and includes land, commercial property and residential property.

Personal property must be exchanged for personal property and the proceeds of the sale must be re-invested in a like kind asset within 180 days of the sale.

Restrictions are imposed on the number of properties which can be identified as potential replacement properties. More than one potential replacement property can be identified as long as you satisfy one of these rules:

The Three-Property Rule - Up to three properties regardless of their market values. All identified properties are not required to be purchased to satisfy the exchange, only the amount needed to satisfy the value requirement.

The 200% Rule - Any number of properties as long as the aggregate fair market value of all replacement properties does not exceed 200% of the aggregate Fair Market Value of all of the relinquished properties as of the initial transfer date. All identified properties are not required to be purchased to satisfy the exchange, only the amount needed to satisfy the value requirement.

The 95% Rule - Any number of replacement properties if the fair market value of the properties actually received by the end of the exchange period is at least 95% of the aggregate fair market value of all the potential replacement properties identified. In other words, 95% (or all) of the properties identified must be purchased or the entire exchange is invalid.

The following sequence represents the order of steps in a typical 1031 exchange:

1. Retain the services of tax counsel/CPA. Become advised by same.

2. Sell the property, including the Cooperation Clause in the sales agreement.

"Buyer is aware that the seller's intention is to complete a 1031 Exchange through this transaction and hereby agrees to cooperate with seller to accomplish same, at no additional cost or liability to buyer."

Make sure your escrow officer/closing agent contacts the Qualified Intermediary to order the exchange documents.

3. Enter into a 1031 exchange agreement with your Qualified Intermediary.

The Qualified Intermediary is named as principal in the sale of your relinquished property and the subsequent purchase of your replacement property.

The 1031 Exchange Agreement must meet IRS Requirements, especially pertaining to the proceeds. Along with the agreement, an amendment to escrow is signed which names the Qualified Intermediary as seller. Normally, the deed is still prepared for recording from the taxpayer to the true buyer. It is not necessary to have the replacement property identified at this time.

4. The sale closes, and the closing statement reflects that the Qualified Intermediary was the seller, and the proceeds go to your Qualified Intermediary.

The funds should be placed in a separate account to insure liquidity and safety. The closing date of the relinquished property escrow is Day 0 of the exchange, and that's when the clock begins to tick.

Written identification of the address of the replacement property must be sent within 45 days and the identified replacement property must be acquired by the taxpayer within 180 days.

5. The taxpayer sends written identification of the address or legal description of the replacement property to the Qualified Intermediary, on or before Day 45.

It must be signed by everyone who signed the exchange

agreement, and it may be faxed, hand delivered, or mailed either to the Qualified Intermediary, the seller of the replacement property or his agent.

Send it via certified mail, return receipt requested. You will then have proof of receipt from a government agency.

6. Taxpayer enters into an agreement to purchase replacement property, again including the Cooperation Clause.

"Seller is aware that the buyer's intention is to complete a 1031 Exchange.

An amendment is signed naming the Qualified Intermediary as buyer, but again, the deeding is from the true seller to the taxpayer.

7. When conditions are satisfied and escrow is prepared to close and certainly prior to the 180th day, per the 1031 Exchange Agreement, the Qualified Intermediary forward the exchange funds and gross proceeds to escrow, and the closing statement reflects the Qualified Intermediary as the buyer. A final accounting is sent by the Qualified Intermediary to the taxpayer, showing the funds coming in from one escrow and going out to the other, all without constructive receipt by the taxpayer.

8. Taxpayer files form 8824 with the IRS when taxes are filed, and whatever similar document(s) your particular state requires.

Appendix C
Purchase Authorization

Documents Required Prior to Investment Funding

Below is the process for funding your real estate investment. This property will be part of your Midland investment portfolio. Incomplete documentation may result in delays.

To be supplied by client to Midland by fax/email/mail:

Real Estate Purchase Authorization — All sections of this form must be completed prior to funding.

Payment Authorization Letter—This authorization gives Midland authority to pay property expenses.

Proof of Hazard Insurance (not required for vacant land) Client can elect out of hazard insurance requirement by sending opt-out letter/email.

Midland will work with closing agent and attorneys to oversee preparation of:

HUD/Settlement Statement

Warranty Deed   Preliminary is accepted.

Title Insurance Commitment   If a title company is not being used, we require a signed declaration from the client, waiving title insurance. It is the client's responsibility to record the deed properly.

IRA Investor's name, address & Tax ID listed as owner:

Midland IRA Inc. FBO Client Name & Account # Client address

Trust Tax ID: 47-5560347

Typical closing timeline:

Closing documents must be sent to Midland for review at least 72 hours before closing.

Midland will send prepared documents to client for approval 48 hours before closing.

Client will initial documents on bottom right-hand corner of each page.

Upon receipt of client approval, Midland will execute and mail all closing documents 24 hours prior to closing.

At close of escrow, Midland must receive the following: Warranty Deed, Title Policy, Closing Statement, Hazard Insurance.

Midland IRA I MidlandIRA.com I V @MidlandIRA I f facebook.com/midlandira Chicago: (312) 235-0300 I Ft. Myers: (239) 333-4452

193

Frequently Asked Questions About Real Estate IRAs

Q: I have found a property that I would like to purchase, what do I do now?

A: Make an offer on the property. The IRA investor is allowed to sign the offer letter. Make sure the buyer's name is listed as "Midland IRA Inc. FBO Your Name, Your Midland Account #."

Q: My offer has been accepted, what do I do now?

A: Have the real estate contract prepared. Remember to make sure the buyer's name is listed correctly as

your IRA. Send Midland the contract, along with Midland's Purchase Authorization Letter (PAL) for review. If earnest money needs to be provided, include that dollar amount in Section 2 of the PAL. If the PAL and contract are in good order, Midland will execute the contract and issue applicable earnest money from the IRA.

Q: Can I get a loan to buy this property?

A: Yes. However, it must be a non-recourse loan. This means that neither you nor your IRA (as the buyer) can personally guarantee the mortgage. The loan can only be secured by the property itself. Most traditional banks do not offer non-recourse loans. Contact our office for more information.

Q: What other options do I have to finance a property?

A: You can partner with yourself or other parties on this transaction. For example, your IRA might contribute 40%, you personally contribute 40% and your business partner contributes 20%. All income and expenses related to the property would be split pro rata, according to the percentages contributed. Each party's ownership would be listed separately as an undivided interest on the Deed and Title policy.

Q: Will there be a representative from Midland at my closing?

A: No. IRA closings are completed similar to trust closings. All documents will be executed by a Midland signatory and sent overnight to the closing agent at least 24 hours prior to closing. As the IRA owner, you may attend a table closing, but it is not necessary as the IRA client has no authority to sign on behalf of Midland ("Buyer").

Real Estate
Purchase Authorization

1.	ACCOUNT INFORMATION

Name: Mr.   Ms.   Mrs.   Dr.   _____

Midland Account Number: _____

2.	PROPERTY DETAIL

Property Address:	
City, State, Zip:	
A.P.N. / Legal Description	
Property Contract Price	Deposit Amount (Must be funded by IRA)
IRA Percentage of Ownership	Will the property be mortgaged?* No (Skip to Section 4) Yes (Please complete Section 3)
*Any mortgage on an IRA owned property must be non-recourse and may subject the IRA to Unrelated Debt Financed Income Tax. For more information consult your tax professional or review IRS publication 598.	

3. LOAN DETAILS (Only applicable if there will be financing involved)

Is this loan Non-Recourse?

Yes   No (Please Contact Midland)

Do we have your authorization to set the mortgage payment up to go out automatically?
Yes   No

Note Face Value

Loan #

Interest Rate   Payment Amount

Frequency of Payments
Monthly Annually Other:

Interest Only, or Amortized

Maturity Date

Date of Month Payment is to be Sent

Lender Name (Checks Made Payable To)

Lender Phone

Lender Address (Payment Mailed To)

4. TITLE COMPANY / ESCROW AGENT

Company Name   Contact Name

Phone Number _____ Fax _____ Email_____

5. PROPERTY MANAGER

A property manager is not required for your IRA owned property; however, it is recommended to name a third party manager should there be a need for immediate payment or repairs, which you and any disqualified party are personally prohibited from providing. This third party manager can provide immediate payment and be reimbursed from the IRA with appropriate authorization and applicable invoice. The IRA owner and any disqualified parties CAN NOT be reimbursed for any expenses paid personally on behalf of the IRA.

Check here if there will not be a third-party property manager		
Name	Address	Phone Number
Signature: _____ Date:_____		

6. **FUNDING INSTRUCTIONS** Please send the funds for purchase		
	WIRE ☐	CHECK TO BE PROVIDED ☐

Brantley

Real Estate
Purchase Authorization

WIRE - Please complete the info below $30 wire fee applies		For CHECK - Please complete the info below Allow additional processing time if sent regular mail Void after 90 days
Bank Name		Make Check Payable To
Account Holder Name		Mail Check To
ABA Routing Number	Account Number	Address
For Credit To		City, State, Zip Send Check via: Regular Mail Overnight Mail ($30) Cashier's Check ($30 + Overnight Fee) Hold for pick-up

7. SIGNATURE AND ACKNOWLEDGEMENT

| UPLOAD: midlandira.com/upload
FAX: (239) 466-5496
EMAIL: mail@midlandira.com
MAIL: Mail to office nearest to you | **CHICAGO OFFICE**
Midland IRA
135 S LaSalle St Ste 2150
Chicago, IL 60603 | **FORT MYERS OFFICE**
Midland IRA
1520 Royal Palm Square Blvd Ste 320
Fort Myers, FL 33919 |

I confirm that I am directing Midland IRA, Administrator, to complete this transaction as specified above. I understand that my account is self-directed, and I take complete responsibility for any investment I choose for my account, including the investment specified in this Purchase Authorization. I understand that neither the Administrator nor the Custodian (Mainstar Trust) sells or endorses any investment products, and that they are not affiliated in any way with any investment provider. I understand that the roles of the Administrator and the Custodian are limited, and their responsibilities do not include investment selection for my account. I acknowledge that neither the Administrator nor the Custodian has provided or assumed responsibility for any tax, legal or investment advice with respect to this investment, and I agree that they will not be liable for any loss which results from my decision to purchase the investment. I understand that neither the Administrator nor the Custodian has reviewed or will review the merits, legitimacy, appropriateness or suitability of this investment, and I certify that I have done my own due diligence investigation prior to instructing the Administrator to make this investment for my account. I understand that neither the Administrator nor the Custodian determines whether this investment is acceptable under the Employee Retirement Income Securities Act (ERISA), the Internal Revenue Code (IRC), or any applicable federal, state, or local laws, including securities laws. I understand that it is my responsibility to review any investments to ensure compliance with these requirements.

I understand that in processing this transaction the Administrator and the Custodian are only acting as my agent, and nothing will be construed as conferring fiduciary status on either the Administrator or the Custodian. I agree that the Administrator and the Custodian will not be liable for any investment losses sustained by me or my account as a result of this transaction. I agree to indemnify and hold harmless the Administrator and the Custodian from any and all claims, damages, liability, actions, costs, expenses (including reasonable attorneys' fees) and any loss to my account as a result of any action taken in connection with this investment transaction or resulting from serving as the Administrator or the Custodian for this investment, including, without limitation, claims, damages, liability, actions and losses asserted by me.

I understand that if this Purchase Authorization and any accompanying documentation are not received as required, or, if received, are unclear in the opinion of the Administrator, or if there is insufficient Undirected Cash in my account to fully comply with my instructions to purchase the investment and to pay all fees, the Administrator may not process this transaction until proper documentation and/or clarification is received, and the Administrator will have no liability for loss of income or appreciation.

I understand that my account is subject to the provisions of Internal Revenue Code (IRC) §4975, which defines certain prohibited transactions. I acknowledge that neither the Administrator nor the Custodian has made or will make any determination as to whether this investment is prohibited under §4975 or under any other federal, state or local law. I certify that making this investment will not constitute a prohibited transaction and that it complies with all applicable federal, state, and local laws, regulations and requirements.

I understand that my account is subject to the provisions of IRC §§511-514 relating to Unrelated Business Taxable Income (UBTI) of tax-exempt organizations.

If this investment generates UBTI, I understand that I will be responsible for preparing or having prepared the required IRS Form 990-T tax return and any other documents that may be required. I understand that neither the Administrator nor the Custodian makes any determination of whether or not investments in my account generate UBTI.

I understand that the assets in my account are required by the IRS to be valued annually as of the end of each calendar year. I agree to provide the prior year end value of this investment by no later than January 10th of each year on a form provided by the Administrator, with substantiation attached to support the value provided.

Brantley

I understand that with some types of accounts there are rules for Required Minimum Distributions (RMDs) from the account. If I am now subject to the RMD rules in my account, or if I will become subject to those rules during the term of this investment, I represent that I have verified either that the investment will provide income or distributions sufficient to cover each RMD, or that there are other assets in my account or in other accounts that are sufficiently liquid (including cash) from which I will be able to withdraw my RMDs. I understand that failure to take RMDs may result in a tax penalty of 50% of the amount I should have withdrawn.

I understand that all communication regarding this transaction must be in writing and must be signed by me or by my authorized agent on my behalf, and that no oral modification of my instructions will be valid.

I understand and agree that neither the Administrator nor the Custodian bears or assumes any responsibility to notify me or to secure or maintain any fire, casualty, liability or other insurance coverage, including but not limited to title insurance coverage, on this investment or on any property which serves as collateral for this investment. I acknowledge and agree that it is my sole responsibility to decide what insurance is necessary or appropriate for

investments in my account, and to direct the Administrator in writing (on a form prescribed by the Administrator) to pay the premiums for any such insurance.

I further understand and agree that neither the Administrator nor the Custodian is responsible for notification or payments of any real estate taxes, homeowners association dues, utilities or other charges with respect to this investment unless I specifically direct the Administrator to pay these amounts in writing (on a form prescribed by the Administrator), and sufficient funds are available to pay these amounts from my account. I acknowledge that it is my responsibility to provide to the Administrator or to ensure that the Administrator has received any and all bills for insurance, taxes, homeowners dues, utilities or other amounts due for this investment. Furthermore, I agree that it is my responsibility to determine that payments have been made by reviewing my account statements.

I understand that no person at the office of the Administrator or the Custodian has the authority to modify any of the foregoing provisions. I certify that I have examined this Purchase Authorization and any accompanying documents or information

Print Name:

Signature: _____ **Date:** _____

Appendix D
Realty Masters of FL Application for Residency

Main Office 4400 Bayou Blvd, Ste #58B, Pensacola, FL 32503 / Phone: 850.473.3983 West Office 6800 W. Hwy 98, Pensacola, FL 32506 / Phone: 850.453.9220

Email Documents to Info@PensacolaRealtyMasters.com or Fax 850.473.3975

THE FOLLOWING POLICIES HAVE BEEN ESTABLISHED TO ENSURE THAT ALL PROSPECTIVE APPLICANTS FOR A PROPERTY ARE PROCESSED BY REALTY MASTERS OF FL AND WILL BE TREATED EQUALLY AND FAIRLY.

APPLICANTS AND APPLICATION FEE

Complete Applications will be processed in the order received. If you feel you meet the guidelines for qualifying, we encourage you to submit an application.

➔ Each person 18 years of age or older residing in the property must complete and sign an application.

→ Each applicant must provide proof of identity with state issued photo ID.

→ $35.00 non-refundable processing fee per applicant. $20.00 non-refundable processing fee for active duty military and spouse. ***CASH OR MONEY ORDER ONLY. NO PERSONAL CHECKS, CREDIT, OR DEBIT CARDS IN OFFICE.*** Application fee can be paid online with debit/ credit card through online application system.

→ Incomplete Applications, as well as applications with missing or false information, will not be considered.

→ If a co-signer is necessary, the co-signer must also complete and sign an application. The acceptance of a co-signer is not normal policy and is subject to individual approval or denial by Owner.

→ Your application will not be considered without a completed and signed application for each adult over the age of 18 as well as a copy of photo ID, most recent month's verifiable proof of income, an application fee for each applicant, and photos of any animals residing in the property. Include these items with your application so your application can be considered complete; incomplete applications will not be processed.

CRITERIA FOR APPROVAL

Where there are co-applicants, owner may deny all co-applicants based on one co-applicants failure to pass criteria.

1. **Minimum acceptable credit score of 600 is required.** Upon completion of application, a credit inquiry will be made. Credit history must not contain judgments, collections, liens or bankruptcy within the past one year. Eviction filing and foreclosures within the last 3 years will be grounds for disqualification.

2. **A minimum of one (1) year residential history is required.** Previous rental history reports from landlords must reflect timely payment, sufficient notice of intent to vacate, no complaints regarding noise or illegal activities, no unpaid NSF checks, no damage to the unit upon move out, and no outstanding monies owed to landlord.

3. **Applicants' combined gross monthly income must be three (3) times the amount of the monthly rent.** Applicant must provide one month's paystubs for verification of income. Self-employed applicants must provide their most recent tax return and three (3) months bank statements.

4. A background check will be completed on each applicant.

PETS AND ASSISTANCE ANIMALS
Pets are accepted on case by case basis with owners' approval and a $250 non-refundable pet fee per pet.

→ It is the sole discretion of the owner to approve or deny for any reason a pet request by the tenant. In order for your pet(s) to be considered, you must complete the pet section on the application and supply current photos with this application.

➔ Due to insurance regulations, we cannot accept Doberman Pinschers, German Shepherds, Pit Bulls, Chows, Rottweilers, Siberian Huskies or any other aggressive breed or mix of an aggressive breed. These policies do not apply to assistance animals.

➔ Assistance animals are welcome with proper documentation from a medical professional. See our assistance animal policy for questions regarding service animals and emotional support animals.

CONDITIONS OF MOVE IN

We cannot hold a property vacant longer than 2 weeks past the receipt of a signed lease; therefore, the lease start date must be no later than two weeks from deposit.

➔ Once approved, applicant must immediately schedule an appointment to sign lease and pay security deposit. Hours for lease signing with a property manager are Monday - Friday from 9 am to 4pm.

➔ All moving in funds are to be paid in certified funds. Security Deposit, $50 Administrative Fee, first (1st) full month's rent, and any applicable pet fees are to be paid in cashier's check or money order before keys are provided - *NO CASH, PERSONAL CHECKS, and DEBIT OR CREDIT CARDS*. Prorated rent, if applicable, is due the first day of the following month. Tenants moving in on the 25th or later require payment of prorated rent, as well as the full month's rent, at the time of move in.

→ All utility accounts must be transferred into the resident's name as of the date of possession.

→ Applicant has read the lease and all addendums and agrees to its terms upon completing application.

→ If you choose to lease a house sight unseen, you will be required to sign a sight unseen addendum. If you are out of the area, we strongly suggest you have a representative view the home in your absence and complete neighborhood research prior to applying or entering into a lease. Any application fees, security deposits, rent, and/or pet fees are nonrefundable should you decide you do not to move forward.

CURRENT RESIDENT(S)

If you currently lease a home through Realty Masters, we will gladly waive your application fee; however, a new application must be submitted with all requested documentation. Tenants must meet all criteria set forth in order to qualify. A new security deposit and new pet fees, if applicable, must be paid at the time of lease signing.

Any exceptions to our policy will need to be submitted in writing for presentation to the owner for consideration. If approval is then given for such exceptions, additional security deposits, co-signers, and/or additional advance rental payments may be required. Our company policy is to report all non-compliance with terms of your rental agreement or failure to pay rent, or any amounts owed to the credit bureau.

ACKNOWLEDGEMENT OF APPLICATION FOR RESIDENCY POLICIES

I/we understand if I am applying with co-applicants, all applicants must complete an application and provide necessary documentation before my application can be considered complete and processed.

By signing below, I/we agree that I/we have read and agree to the Application for Residency policies and attest all information presented to be true and accurate. I/we authorize my application to be processed once completed:

Applicant #1 Signature	Date	Print Name Clearly

Applicant #2 Signature	Date	Print Name Clearly

Property Applying for: _____

Desired Move-In Date: _____

I/we have included the following documents with my/our application(s):

Appl. #1 Appl. #2 (Please X if attached)

☐ ☐   Copy of Photo ID

☐ ☐   One Month's verifiable proof of income or 3 month's bank statements and last year's tax return Documented sources of any and all income to be used in consideration for approval

☐ ☐   A $35 application fee per adult ($20 active
☐ ☐   duty military & spouse)

Photos of any animals residing in the property

APPLICANT 1 INFORMATION -Must supply copy of driver's license	
Applicant Name :	Alias:
Date of Birth:	Social Security #
Driver's License #	State: Exp.
Best Phone #	E-mail:
Auto Year: Make: Model:	State/License plate #

CURRENT RESIDENCY INFORMATION – Must provide landlord contact info if applicable	
Current Address:	City, State, Zip:
Do you: ☐ Rent ☐ Own Since when?	Current Rent: $
Landlords Name: Phone #	Email:

Reason for leaving:	How long at this address?
Have you given notice to vacate? ☐ Yes ☐ No	Move out date:
Do you have renters insurance? ☐ Yes ☐ No	If No, Will you get renters insurance? ☐ Yes ☐ No

PREVIOUS RESIDENCY INFORMATION

Previous Address:	City, State, Zip:
Landlords Name: Phone #	Email:
How long at this address?	Reason for leaving:

INCOME INFORMATION –Must provide 1 month's proof of income or tax return & 3 months bank statements

Employer: How long at job?		Phone #
Monthly Income: $ Position:		Other Income: $

Explain any other income:	
Previous Employer: How long at job?	Phone #

REFERENCES	
Personal Reference Name	Address:
Relationship to you:	Phone#
Emergency Contact Name:	Address:
Relationship to you:	Phone #

APPLICANT 1, PLEASE ANSWER THE FOLLOWING	
Have you ever had an eviction? ☐ Yes ☐ No When?	Have you had a foreclosure? ☐ Yes ☐ No When?

Have you ever willfully and intentionally refused to pay any rent when due? ☐ Yes ☐ No

Explain:

Have you ever filed a petition of bankruptcy? ☐ Yes ☐ No If yes, when and what type?

Do you plan to run a business in the residence? ☐ Yes ☐ No Please explain:

Have you or any members of your household ever been convicted of, plead guilty or no contest to, any felony criminal offense or had any felony criminal offense other than a traffic infraction with a disposition other than by acquittal or a finding of not guilty?

☐ Yes ☐ No

Have you or any members of your household ever been convicted of, plead guilty or no contest to, a felony for manufacturing, selling, and/or distributing drugs, causing bodily harm to another, or property crimes including but not limited to arson or property damage within the past seven (7) years? ☐ Yes ☐ No

Have you or any members of your household ever been convicted of, plead guilty or no contest to a sexual related offense or are a registered sex offender? ☐ Yes ☐ No

If yes to any of the foregoing, please provide written details for each conviction showing what court in which the plea or verdict was entered and include the charges you were convicted of, pled guilty or no contest to, the date of such conviction, and describe the punishment given. _____

CO-APPLICANTS - ALL ADULTS OVER THE AGE OF 18 MUST COMPLETE APPLICATION AND SUBMIT DOCUMENTS

Are you applying with other occupants? ☐ Yes ☐ No If yes, complete:	Name:

Name:	Name:

CHILDREN OCCUPYING THE PREMISES	
Total number of children living with you under age of 18?	
Name Age	Name Age
Name Age	Name Age
Name Age	Name Age

HOUSEHOLD PET INFORMATION – photos must be provided of each pet	
Total number of pets in your household?	Name Age Weight

Type	Breed	Color	Name	Age	Weight
Type	Breed	Color	Name	Age	Weight
Type	Breed	Color	Are your pets up to date on vaccines? ☐ Yes ☐ No		
Are your pets registered with the city/county? ☐ Yes ☐ No					

ASSISTANCE ANIMALS

Do you have a service or emotional support animal? ☐ Yes ☐ No
If yes, complete below:

Type	Breed	Color	Name	Age	Weight
Type	Breed	Color	Name	Age	Weight

If yes, do you have a letter from a medical professional to provide with application?
☐ Yes ☐ No

If additional applicant(s), please complete the following:

APPLICANT 2 INFORMATION - Must supply copy of driver's license	
Applicant Name:	Alias:
Date of Birth:	Social Security #
Driver's License #	State: Exp.
Best Phone #	E-mail:
Auto Year: Make: Model:	State/License plate #

CURRENT RESIDENCY INFORMATION – Must provide landlord contact info if applicable	
Current Address:	City, State, Zip:
Do you: ☐ Rent ☐ Own Since when?	Current Rent: $
Landlords Name: Phone #	Email:
Reason for leaving:	How long at this address?

Have you given notice to vacate? ☐ Yes ☐ No	Move out date:
Do you have renters insurance? ☐ Yes ☐ No	If No, Will you get renters insurance? ☐ Yes ☐ No

PREVIOUS RESIDENCY INFORMATION	
Previous Address:	City, State, Zip:
Landlords Name: Phone #	Email:
How long at this address?	Reason for leaving:

INCOME INFORMATION –Must provide 1 month's proof of income or tax return & 3 months bank statements	
Employer: How long at job?	Phone #
Monthly Income: $ Position:	Other Income: $
Explain any other income:	
Previous Employer: How long at job?	Phone #

REFERENCES	
Personal Reference Name	Address:
Relationship to you:	Phone#
Emergency Contact Name:	Address:
Relationship to you:	Phone #

APPLICANT 2, PLEASE ANSWER THE FOLLOWING	
Have you ever had an eviction? ☐ Yes ☐ No When?	Have you had a foreclosure? ☐ Yes ☐ No When?
Have you ever willfully and intentionally refused to pay any rent when due? ☐ Yes ☐ No Explain:	
Have you ever filed a petition of bankruptcy? ☐ Yes ☐ No If yes, when and what type?	
Do you plan to run a business in the residence? ☐ Yes ☐ No Please explain:	

Have you or any members of your household ever been convicted of, plead guilty or no contest to, any felony criminal offense or had any felony criminal offense other than a traffic infraction with a disposition other than by acquittal or a finding of not guilty?

☐ Yes ☐ No

Have you or any members of your household ever been convicted of, plead guilty or no contest to, a felony for manufacturing, selling, and/or distributing drugs, causing bodily harm to another, or property crimes including but not limited to arson or property damage within the past seven (7) years? ☐ Yes ☐ No

Have you or any members of your household ever been convicted of, plead guilty or no contest to a sexual related offense or are a registered sex offender? ☐ Yes ☐ No

If yes to any of the foregoing, please provide written details for each conviction showing what court in which the plea or verdict was entered and include the charges you were convicted of, pled guilty or no contest to, the date of such conviction, and describe the punishment given. _____

_____

Are you currently on probation or parole? ☐ Yes ☐ No

Please provide written details for any additional information or explanation as to the circumstance surrounding such conviction or efforts of rehabilitation, if applicable, that you want to provide. Failure to provide the written specifics will result in your application being incomplete and therefore, will not be processed.

APPLICATION AUTHORIZATION & CONSENT FOR RELEASE OF INFORMATION

Applicants represent that all of the statements and representations submitted to Realty Masters during the application process are true and complete and hereby authorize verification of the above references and credit records. Applicant understands that an investigative consumer report including information about any character, credit history, general reputation, personal characteristics, mode of living, and all public record information including criminal records may be made.

Applicant agrees that false, misleading or misrepresented information may result in the application being rejected, will void my lease/rental agreement if any and/or be grounds for immediate eviction with loss of all deposits and any other penalties as provided by the lease terms if any.

Applicant authorizes verification of all information by Realty Masters. Applicant has the right to make a written request within a reasonable period of time to receive additional, detailed information about the nature and scope of this investigation.

NON REFUNDABLE APPLICATION FEE-Applicant(s) has paid to Landlord and or Management company herewith the sum of $ as a NON REFUNDABLE APPLICATION FEE for costs, expenses and fees in processing the application.

Once approved, a $50 Administrative Fee and Security Deposit is due and must be paid with certified funds. Realty Masters does not take the property off the market until a security deposit is in place.

SECURITY DEPOSIT AGREEMENT: Security deposits are only to be paid after a completed application has been approved. If Applicant has deposited a "SECURITY DEPOSIT" of $ i   n consideration for taking the dwelling off the market, applicant agrees to move in the property within 2 weeks of receipt of the paid security deposit. If applicant is approved but fails to enter into the lease within 3 days of verbal and/or written approval and or take possession after lease signing, the FULL "SECURITY DEPOSIT" shall be forfeited to the Landlord or Management. Keys will be furnished only after lease and other rental documents have been properly executed by all parties, and only after all applicable rental fees have been paid, including first full month's rent and pet fees when applicable.

Realty Masters of FL is an equal opportunity housing provider and does not discriminate on the basis of race or color, age, religion, sex, national origin, familial status, or disability.

I HAVE READ AND AGREE TO THE PROVISIONS AS STATED.

_____   _____
Applicant #1 Signature   Date

_____
Print Name Clearly

_____   _____
Applicant #2 Signature   Date

_____
Print Name Clearly

Appendix E
Application Denial Letter

Date: _____

Applicant Name(s): _____

Thank you for applying at (Rental Address) _____

_____:

Regretfully, your application to rent the above described premises was not approved for one or more of the following reasons:

( ) Incomplete application, inaccurate or false information or unable to verify information provided by the applicant.

( ) Insufficient income or debt to income ratio to meet qualifying standard.

( ) Information was received from a person or company other than a consumer reporting agency. Under Section 315(b) of the Fair Credit Reporting Act you have a right to make a written request to us within 60 days of receiving this letter for a disclosure of the nature of this information.

( ) Adverse history of damage to other rental properties, references regarding relations with neighbors.

( ) Information was received from (name, address telephone

<u>and toll free telephone of provider</u>). (<u>name of provider</u>) did not make the decision to take this adverse action and is unable to provide the specific reasons why the adverse action was taken. You have a right to obtain a free copy of a report by making demand on the provider within 60 days of your receipt of this letter. You also have a right to dispute with the provider the accuracy or completeness of any consumer report furnished by them. You have certain rights under federal law regarding your credit history.

During the sixty-day period that starts now, you have the right to receive a free copy of your consumer report from the consumer reporting agency marked above. That disclosure can be made orally, in writing, or electronically.

You have a right to dispute the accuracy or completeness of any information contained in your consumer report, as furnished by the consumer reporting agency whose name is checked off above. If you believe your file contains errors, is inaccurate or incomplete, call the consumer reporting agency at their toll free number listed above, or write to them at the address listed.

You may have additional rights under the credit reporting or consumer protection laws of your state. Contact your state or local consumer protection agency or a state Attorney General's office.

Sincerely

_____

Landlord/Agent

Appendix F
REALTY MASTERS
RESIDENTIAL LEASE

1. This agreement, made this _____ day of   between _____ hereinafter referred to as the LANDLORD, through its AGENT Realty Masters and_____,hereinafter referred to as the TENANT, concerning the lease of the following described property: _____

2. _____, is agreed to by and shall bind the TENANT, its heirs, estate, or legally appointed representatives. TENANT as herein used shall include all persons to whom this property is leased. LANDLORD as herein used shall include the owner(s) of the premises, its heirs, assigns or representatives and/or any agent(s) designated by the owner(s).

3. **LEGAL DESCRIPTION OF PROPERTY:** _____

4. **TERMS OF LEASE:** _____ **Total Rental Amount for lease terms: $**_____ **Monthly Rental Amount $**_____ **Beginning** _____ **Ending** _____ If for any reason LANDLORD cannot deliver possession of the premises to TENANT by the beginning date, the lease may be voided at LANDLORD'S option without LANDLORD being liable for any expenses caused by such delay or termination. This lease shall terminate early, at LANDLORD'S option, upon sale of or contract for sale entered into on the premises and TENANT agrees to vacate within 60 days written notice from LANDLORD.

5. **OCCUPANTS:** Only the following individuals shall occupy the premises unless written consent of the LANDLORD is obtained:_____ A reasonable number of guests may occupy the premises without prior written consent if stay is limited to 14 days.

6. **PRORATED RENT:** TENANT agrees to pay the sum of $ as prorated rent for the period .

7. **ADVANCE RENT:** TENANT agrees to pay the sum of   as advance rent representing payment for the last month of lease term.

8. **RENT: TENANT agrees to pay the monthly rent amount of $ plus any applicable sales tax as rent on the 1st day of each month in advance without demand at Realty Masters, 4400 Bayou Blvd, Ste #58, Pensacola, Florida 32503- Phone # 850-473-3983 Emergency # 850-512-6019. Rent must be received by LANDLORD or its designated agent on or before the due date. Rent is due on the 1st day of each month (the "due date"). If rent is not received on or by the 3rd day, a late fee of 10% of the rent will be assessed on the 4thday of the month. After the 4th day of the month, an additional $5.00 per day thereafter shall be due as additional rent if TENANT fails to make rent payments on or by the 3rd day of each month. All late rent payments must be made with certified funds only._____(Initial).** Cash payments are NOT accepted. Partial payments are NOT accepted. Post-dated checks are not accepted. Rent must be paid by one personal check only or multiple money orders. Only personal checks from parties on the lease will be accepted. If TENANT'S check is dishonored, all future payments must be made in money order or cashier's check; dishonored checks will be subject to the greatest of 5% of the check amount or a $30.00 charge as additional rent. Time is of the essence. The imposition of late fees and/or dishonored check charges are not a substitution or waiver of available

Florida law remedies. If rent is not received by the 1st day of each month, LANDLORD may serve a THREE-DAY notice on the next day or any day thereafter as allowed by law. All signatories to this lease are jointly and severally responsible for the faithful performance of this lease. All payments made shall first be applied to any outstanding balances of any kind including late charges and/or any other charges due under this lease. All notices by TENANT to LANDLORD shall be sent to LANDLORD'S address above by certified mail.

9. **PETS: TENANT shall not keep any animal or pet in or around the rental premises without LANDLORD'S prior written approval and a PET ADDENDUM signed by all parties. See Pet Addendum to lease.**

10. **SECURITY DEPOSIT:** TENANT agrees to pay LANDLORD the sum of $_____ as security for faithful performance by TENANT of all terms, covenants, and conditions of this lease. This deposit may be applied by the LANDLORD for any monies owed by TENANT under the lease or Florida law, including physical damages to the premises, costs, and attorney's fees associated with TENANT'S failure to fulfill the terms of the lease. TENANT cannot dictate that this deposit be used for any rent due. TENANT will still be responsible for unpaid rent, physical damages, future rent due, attorney's fees, costs and any other amounts due under the terms of the lease or Florida law. The security deposit (and advance rent, if applicable) will be held in the following manner: Deposited in a separate non-interest bearing account at _____ in Pensacola, FL.

11. Florida Statutes §83.49(2)(d) provides:

YOUR LEASE REQUIRES PAYMENT OF CERTAIN DEPOSITS. THE LANDLORD MAY TRANSFER ADVANCE RENTS TO THE LANDLORD'S ACCOUNT AS THEY ARE DUE AND WITHOUT NOTICE. WHEN YOU MOVE OUT, YOU MUST GIVE THE

LANDLORD YOUR NEW ADDRESS SO THAT THE LANDLORD CAN SEND YOU NOTICES REGARDING YOUR DEPOSIT. THE LANDLORD MUST MAIL YOU NOTICE, WITHIN 30 DAYS AFTER YOU MOVE OUT, OF THE LANDLORD'S INTENT TO IMPOSE A CLAIM AGAINST THE DEPOSIT. IF YOU DO NOT REPLY TO THE LANDLORD STATING YOUR OBJECTION TO THE CLAIM WITHIN 15 DAYS AFTER RECEIPT OF THE LANDLORD'S NOTICE, THE LANDLORD WILL COLLECT THE CLAIM AND MUST MAIL YOU THE REMAINING DEPOSIT, IF ANY.

IF THE LANDLORD FAILS TO TIMELY MAIL YOU NOTICE, THE LANDLORD MUST RETURN THE DEPOSIT BUT MAY LATER FILE A LAWSUIT AGAINST YOU FOR DAMAGES. IF YOU FAIL TO TIMELY OBJECT TO A CLAIM, THE LANDLORD MAY COLLECT FROM THE DEPOSIT, BUT YOU MAY LATER FILE A LAWSUIT CLAIMING A REFUND.

YOU SHOULD ATTEMPT TO INFORMALLY RESOLVE ANY DISPUTE BEFORE FILING A LAWSUIT. GENERALLY, THE PARTY IN WHOSE FAVOR A JUDGMENT IS RENDERED WILL BE AWARDED COSTS AND ATTORNEY FEES PAYABLE BY THE LOSING PARTY.

THIS DISCLOSURE IS BASIC. PLEASE REFER TO PART II OF CHAPTER 83, FLORIDA STATUTES, TO DETERMINE YOUR LEGAL RIGHTS AND OBLIGATIONS.

12. Florida Statutes §83.49(3) provides:

a. Upon the vacating of the premises for termination of the lease if the landlord does not intend to impose a claim on the security deposit, the landlord shall have 15 days to return the security deposit together with interest if otherwise required, or the landlord shall have 30 days to give the tenant written notice by certified mail to the tenant's last known mailing address of his or her intention to impose a claim on the deposit and the reason for imposing the claim. The notice shall contain a statement in substantially the following form:

This is a notice of my intention to impose a claim for damages in the amount of .... upon your security deposit, due to ..... It is sent to you as required by s. 83.49(3), Florida Statutes. You are hereby notified that you must object in writing to this deduction from your security deposit within 15 days from the time you receive this notice or I will be authorized to deduct my claim from your security deposit. Your objection must be sent to ... (landlord's address) ....

If the landlord fails to give the required notice within the 30-day period, he or she forfeits the right to impose a claim upon the security deposit and may not seek a setoff against the deposit but may file an action for damages after return of the deposit.

b. Unless the tenant objects to the imposition of the landlord's claim or the amount thereof within 15 days after receipt of the landlord's notice of intention to impose a claim, the landlord may then deduct the amount of his or her claim and shall remit the balance of the deposit to the tenant within 30 days after the date of the notice of intention to impose a claim for damages. The failure of the tenant to make a timely objection does not waive any rights of the tenant to seek damages in a separate action.

c. If either party institutes an action in a court of competent jurisdiction to adjudicate the party's right to the security deposit, the prevailing party is entitled to receive his or her court costs plus a reasonable fee for his or her attorney. The court shall advance the cause on the calendar.

d. Compliance with this section by an individual or business entity authorized to conduct business in this state, including Florida-licensed real estate brokers and sales associates, constitutes compliance with all other relevant Florida Statutes pertaining to security deposits held pursuant to a rental agreement or other landlord-tenant relationship. Enforcement personnel shall look solely to this section to determine compliance. This section prevails over any conflicting provisions in chapter 475 and in other sections of the Florida Statutes, and shall operate to permit licensed real estate brokers to disburse security deposits and deposit money without having to comply with the notice and settlement procedures contained in s. 475.25(1)(d).

13. **Security deposit refunds if any shall be made by mail only, as provided by law, made out in names of all TENANTS in one check, and, may not be picked up in person from LANDLORD.**

14. **ASSIGNMENTS:** TENANT shall not assign this lease or sublet the premises or any part thereof. Any unauthorized transfer of interest by the TENANT shall be a breach of this agreement.

15. **APPLICATION:** If TENANT has filled out a rental application, any misrepresentation made by the TENANT in same will be a breach of this agreement and LANDLORD may terminate the tenancy.

16. **FIXTURES AND ALTERATIONS:** TENANT must obtain prior written consent from LANDLORD before painting, installing fixtures, making alterations, additions or improvements, and if permission is granted, the same shall become LANDLORD'S property and shall remain on the premises at the termination of the tenancy.

17. **USE OF PREMISES:** TENANT shall maintain the premises in a clean and sanitary condition and not disturb surrounding residents or the peaceful and quiet enjoyment of the premises or surrounding premises. TENANT shall install window shades or draperies (no foil, sheets, paper etc. allowed) within 15 days of taking occupancy if not already provided. Premises are to be used and occupied by the TENANT for only residential, non-business, private housing

purposes only. TENANT shall not operate any type of day care or child sitting service on the premises. **TENANT shall secure insurance immediately for any water filled devices with a loss payable clause to LANDLORD. Tenant shall not be allowed to have large above ground pools or trampolines on the premises.**_____ **(Initial). Lawn & shrub maintenance is the tenant's responsibility to properly water and maintain. Failure to regularly service them will result in a professional lawn care company being hired at the tenant's expense for the remainder of the time they reside in the property.**_____ **(Initial)**

18. **NO SMOKING INSIDE OF THE HOME: TENANT agrees there is to be NO SMOKING inside of the premises at any time!**

19. **RISK OF LOSS:** All TENANT'S personal property shall be at the risk of the TENANT or owner thereof and LANDLORD shall not be liable for any damage to said personal property of the TENANT arising from criminal acts, fire, storm, flood, rain or wind damage, acts of negligence of any person whomsoever or from the bursting or leaking of water pipes. TENANT is strongly urged to secure insurance for personal property.

20. **DEFAULT:** (1) Failure of TENANT to pay rent or any additional rent when due, or (2) TENANT'S violation of any other term, condition or covenant of this lease (and if applicable, attached rules and regulations), condominium by-laws or neighborhood deed restrictions or (3) failure of TENANT to comply with any Federal, State and/or County laws, rules ordinances, or (4) TENANT'S failure to move into the premises or tenant's abandonment of the premises, shall constitute a -default by the TENANT. Upon default, rent due for the remaining term of this lease is accelerated, TENANT shall owe this rent and LANDLORD may begin eviction procedures, after proper notice is given under Florida law. TENANT will still be responsible for any unpaid rent, physical damages to the premises, unpaid late fees, attorney's fees,

costs, and any other amounts due under the terms of this lease or Florida law. If the TENANT abandons or surrenders possession of the premises during the lease term or any renewals or is evicted by the LANDLORD, LANDLORD may retake possession of the premises and make a good faith effort to re-rent it for the TENANT account. Retaking of possession shall not constitute a recission of this lease nor a surrender of the leasehold estate.

21. **LITIGATION:** In any litigation between the parties to this agreement that is based on, arises out of, or is in any way related to this agreement, the transaction described herein, or the relationship between the parties as a result of this agreement (referred to herein as "Litigation"), the following provisions shall apply:

a. **Limitation of Liability (Contractual Economic Loss Rule):** LANDLORD and TENANT agree that in any Litigation, neither party shall be liable for any special, indirect, incidental, or consequential damages or any economic damages of any kind that arise in tort; the parties understanding and agreeing that only contract damages shall be recoverable in any claim.

b. **Venue:** In any Litigation, the parties agree that such Litigation shall be brought only in Escambia County, Florida, if in state court or in the Northern District of Florida if in federal court.

c. **JURY TRIAL WAIVER: THE PARTIES UNDERSTAND THAT THEY MAY HAVE A RIGHT TO A JURY TRIAL AS TO CERTAIN CLAIMS THAT COULD ARISE BETWEEN THEM. IN THE EVENT OF ANY LITIGATION, THE PARTIES KNOWINGLY, VOLUNTARILY, AND INTENTIONALLY WAIVE ANY RIGHT THAT THEY MAY HAVE TO A JURY TRIAL. _____ (INITIAL).**

d. **CLASS ACTION WAIVER: THE PARTIES UNDERSTAND THAT THEY MAY HAVE A RIGHT TO BE PARTY TO A CLASS ACTION**

OR REPRESENTATIVE ACTION AS TO CERTAIN CLAIMS THAT COULD ARISE BETWEEN THEM. IN THE EVENT OF ANY LITIGATION, AND TO THE EXTENT ALLOWED BY LAW, THE PARTIES EACH WAIVE ANY RIGHT TO PURSUE DISPUTES ON A CLASSWIDE BASIS; THAT IS, TO EITHER JOIN A CLAIM WITH THE CLAIM OF ANY OTHER PERSON OR ENTITY, OR ASSERT A CLAIM IN A REPRESENTATIVE CAPACITY ON BEHALF OF ANYONE ELSE IN ANY LAWSUIT, ARBITRATION, OR OTHER PROCEEDING. THE PARTY'S ACKNOWLEDGE AND AGREE THAT ANY CLAIMS MUST BE BROUGHT IN THE RESPECTIVE PARTY'S INDIVIDUAL CAPACITY, AND NOT AS A CLASS MEMBER IN ANY PURPORTED CLASS, COLLECTIVE, REPRESENTATIVE, MULTIPLE PLAINTIFF, OR SIMILAR PROCEEDING ("CLASS ACTION"). THE PARTIES KNOWINGLY, VOLUNTARILY, AND INTENTIONALLY WAIVE ANY RIGHT TO BRING OR MAINTAIN ANY CLASS ACTION IN ANY FORUM. _____ (INITIAL).

e. **Attorney Fee Provision:** The parties agree that in the event of any dispute between them that is based on, arises out of, or is in any way related to this agreement, the transaction described herein, or the relationship between the parties as a result of this agreement, and regardless of whether or not a lawsuit is filed, if either party is required to hire an attorney to enforce any of its rights under the terms of this agreement, it shall be entitled to recover it's reasonable attorneys' fees and costs from the other party, including appellate attorneys' fees and costs.

22. **UTILITIES:** LANDLORD is responsible for providing the following utilities only: _____ .The TENANT agrees to pay all charges and deposits for all other utilities and TENANT agrees to have all accounts for utilities immediately placed in TENANT name with accounts kept current throughout occupancy. If the utilities which TENANT is responsible for are still in LANDLORD'S name at the time TENANT takes

occupancy, TENANT agrees that LANDLORD shall order such utilities to be terminated.

23. **VEHICLES:** Vehicle(s) located on the leased premises must be currently licensed, owned by TENANT, registered, operational, and properly marked. TENANT agrees to abide by all parking rules established now or in the future by LANDLORD or condo/homeowner association's rules if applicable. No trailers, campers, vehicles on blocks, motorcycles, boats, or commercial vehicles are allowed on or about the premises without LANDLORD'S prior written approval. TENANT is not to repair or disassemble vehicles on the premises. Vehicles not meeting the above requirements and additional rules of the LANDLORD are unauthorized vehicles subject to being towed at TENANT expense. Parking on the grass is prohibited. TENANT agrees to indemnify LANDLORD for any expenses incurred due to the towing of any vehicle belonging to TENANT or the guests or invitees of TENANT. **TENANT agrees that only the following vehicles will be parked on the premises: _____**

24. **MAINTENANCE/INSPECTION: TENANT agrees that they have fully inspected the premises and accepts the condition of the premises in "as is" condition with no warranties or promises express or implied. TENANT shall maintain the premises in good, clean and tenantable condition throughout the tenancy, keep all plumbing fixtures in good repair, use all electrical, plumbing, heating, cooling, appliances and other equipment in a reasonable manner, removing all garbage in a clean sanitary manner.** If there is a microwave, garbage disposal, icemaker, washer, dryer, ceiling fan, whirlpool, or Jacuzzi present at the home, these items are accepted in as-is condition and are not the LANDLORD'S responsibility to maintain or replace. The Tenant must notify the LANDLORD through the Property Management Company before any of these items

are removed or repaired. Should the Tenant wish to have maintenance done to these items at their cost, a licensed and insured maintenance company must be used and a copy of the paid invoice will be provided to the LANDLORD through the Property Management Company for the LANDLORD'S records. In the event TENANT or TENANT'S guests or invitees cause any damage to the premises, LANDLORD may at its option repair same and TENANT shall pay for the expenses of same on demand or LANDLORD may require TENANT repair same, all charges incurred as additional rent. **TENANT shall be fully responsible for, and agrees to maintain and repair at the TENANT'S expense, unless stated otherwise herein, the following: A/C FILTERS, EXTERMINATION, LAWN/SHRUBBERY, LOCKS/KEYS, SCREENING, AND SMOKE ALARM(S)._____(Initial). In the event a major repair to the premises must be made which will necessitate the TENANT'S vacating the premises, LANDLORD may at its option terminate this agreement and TENANT agrees to vacate the premise holding LANDLORD harmless for any damages suffered if any. TENANT shall IMMEDIATELY notify LANDLORD in writing of any maintenance needed, maintenance performed, or repairs. TENANT agrees that they shall immediately test the smoke detector and shall maintain same.**

25. **VACATING: AT the expiration of this agreement or any extension, TENANT shall peaceably surrender the premises and turn in all keys and any other property owned by LANDLORD leaving the premises in good, clean condition, ordinary wear and tear excepted. TENANT agrees to have the carpeting cleaned professionally by a Realty Masters Approved Vendor, who is licensed and insured, upon move out, and to provide LANDLORD with a receipt for such professional carpet cleaning, or TENANT will incur a minimum carpet cleaning charge of $75.00. In the event all keys are not returned upon move out, there will be a**

minimum charge of $40.00. If home is not clean per tenant handbook move out guidelines, a professional cleaning company will be sent to the property and TENANT agrees to cleaning company charges. If Tenant vacates and leaves the property in a condition that requires LANDLORD to make repairs and/or clean the premises because of Tenant's actions, Tenant shall be charged a $75.00 fee for the expense of the utilities required to make such repairs or clean the premises.

26. **NOTICES AT END OF LEASE TERM:** If TENANT intends to vacate at the end of the lease term, TENANT shall notify LANDLORD in writing not less than 30 days prior to the end of the lease term. If LANDLORD intends not to renew the tenancy at the end of the lease term, LANDLORD shall notify TENANT in writing not less than 30 days prior to the end of the lease term.

27. **RENEWAL/EXTENSION OF TENANCY:** If LANDLORD consents to TENANT remaining in the premises after the natural expiration of this lease and no new lease is signed, the tenancy will be extended as a month-to-month tenancy. A month-to-month tenancy may be terminated by TENANT giving written notice not less than 30 days prior to the end of any monthly payment period OR by LANDLORD giving written notice not less than30 days prior to the end of any monthly payment period, in which eventTermination of the tenancy shall occur on the last day of the month. Failure to give this written notice to LANDLORD will cause TENANT to continue to be bound by the terms of this lease on a month-to-month basis until TENANT gives LANDLORD written notice of termination not less than 30 days prior to the end of any monthly payment period. If TENANT fails to sign a lease renewal timely, the monthly rental amount due from TENANT on a month-to-month basis shall be an amount equal to the market rate at the time of lease expiration, in addition to a $50.00 month-to-month fee. Notice from TENANT

to LANDLORD must be made by certified mail. All other conditions of this lease shall remain in effect. If TENANT fails to vacate after the initial term, or any successive consensual periods after the initial term, TENANT shall additionally be held liable for holdover (double) rent.

28. **RIGHT OF ENTRY:** LANDLORD, upon reasonable notice by telephone, hand-delivery, or posting to TENANT, has the right of entry to the premises for showing, repairs, appraisals, inspections, or any other reason. When performing inspections of the premises, LANDLORD has the right to take photographs of the property, inside and outside, in order to document the condition of the property. LANDLORD has immediate right of entry in cases of emergency, or to protect or preserve the premises. LANDLORD has the right to perform drive-by inspections at any time and without notice. When performing drive-by inspections, LANDLORD may knock on the door of the property or leave a door hanger. TENANT shall not alter or add locks without prior written consent. If consent is given, TENANT must provide LANDLORD with a key to all locks. LANDLORD may place "For Sale" or "For Rent" signs on the premises at any time. In the event LANDLORD gives notice to TENANT for an inspection, for whatever purpose, and the TENANT has changed the locks without consent of LANDLORD or leaves pets out so the inspection cannot be completed, TENANT shall be charged $35.00 for each trip required to conduct such inspection. This fee shall be considered additional rent hereunder.

29. **CONDEMNATION, DAMAGE TO PREMISES, ACTS OF GOD and TERMINATION:** If for any reason the premises are condemned by any governmental authority, destroyed, rendered uninhabitable, rendered dangerous to persons or property, and/or damaged through fire, water, smoke, wind, flood, act of God, nature or accident, or if it becomes necessary, in the opinion of LANDLORD or its agent, that TENANT must vacate the premises in order for repairs to the

premises to be undertaken, this lease shall, at LANDLORD'S option and upon 7 days written notice to TENANT, terminate and TENANT, if not in default of the lease, shall owe no further rent due under the terms of the lease. In such case, TENANT hereby waives all claims against LANDLORD for any damages suffered as a result of such condemnation, damage, destruction, or lease termination.

30. **FORECLOSURE:** In the event that a Certificate of Title is issued as a result of the occurrence of a foreclosure sale with respect to the subject property, this lease may be terminated by either party and neither shall be held liable for any resulting damages. The filing of a foreclosure action against the LANDLORD does not give TENANT the right to terminate the lease; rather, the TENANT'S right to terminate the lease shall be conditioned upon the issuance of a Certificate of Title with respect to the subject property.

31. **WAIVERS:** The rights of the LANDLORD under this lease shall be cumulative, and failure on the part of the LANDLORD to exercise promptly any rights given hereunder shall not operate to forfeit any other rights allowed by this lease or by law.

32. **INDEMNIFICATION: TENANT agrees to reimburse LANDLORD upon demand in the amount of the loss, property damage, or cost of repairs or service, (including plumbing trouble) caused by the negligence or improper use by TENANT, his agents, family or guests.** TENANT at all times, will indemnify and hold harmless LANDLORD for all losses, damages, liabilities, and expenses which can be claimed against LANDLORD for any injuries or damages to the person or property of any persons, caused by the acts, omissions, neglect, or fault of TENANT, his agents, family or guests, or arising from TENANT'S failure to comply with any applicable laws, statutes, ordinances or regulations. In the event of a dispute concerning the tenancy created by this

agreement, TENANT agrees that if the premises are being managed by an agent for the record owner TENANT agrees to hold agent, its successors, employees, and assigns harmless and shall look solely to the record owner of the premises in the event of a legal dispute concerning the tenancy or the security deposit. _____(Initial)

33. **INTEGRATION:** This lease and exhibits, addenda, and attachments, if any, set forth the entire agreements between LANDLORD and TENANT concerning the premises, and there are no covenants, promises, agreements, conditions, or understandings, oral or written between them other than those herein set forth. If any provision in this agreement is illegal, invalid or unenforceable, that provision shall be void but all other terms and conditions of this agreement shall be in effect.

34. **MODIFICATIONS:** No subsequent alteration, amendment, change or addition to this lease shall be binding upon LANDLORD unless reduced to writing and signed by the parties.

35. **RADON GAS:** State law requires the following notice to be given: "Radon is a naturally occurring radioactive gas that, when it has accumulated in a building in sufficient quantities, may present health risks to persons who are exposed to it over time. Levels of radon that exceed federal and state guidelines have been found in buildings in Florida. Additional information regarding radon and radon testing may be obtained from your county public health unit."

36. **TENANT HANDBOOK.** Tenant has received a copy of the Tenant Handbook, which is incorporated into and made a part of this rental agreement.

37. **ABANDONED PROPERTY: BY SIGNING THIS RENTAL AGREEMENT, THE TENANT AGREES THAT UPON**

SURRENDER OR ABANDMONMENT, AS DEFINED BY THE FLORIDA STATUES, THE LANDLORD SHALL NOT BE LIABLE OR RESPONSIBLE FOR STORAGE OR DISPOSITION OF THE TENANT'S PERSONAL PROPERTY.

38. **ADDITIONAL STIPULATIONS: Please check all that apply. The terms of any of the below additional stipulations/ addendums that are checked are incorporated into and made a part of this lease.**

☐ No Smoking/Drug &Crime Free Addendum

Initial_____

☐ Smoke Detector Agreement

Initial_____

☐ Privacy Policy Notice

Initial_____

☐ Security Deposit Agreement

Initial_____

☐ Mold Addendum

Initial_____

☐ Tenant Maintenance Responsibilities

Initial_____

☐ Tenant Handbook & Move-in Inspection Sheet

Initial_____

☐ Pet Addendum

Initial_____

☐ Military Clause

Initial_____

☐ HUD Addendum

Initial_____

☐ Lead Based Paint Form

Initial_____

☐ Santa Rosa County Airport Zone Disclosure Form

Initial_____

☐ Escambia County Airport/Airfield Environs
Real Estate Sale/Lease Disclosure

Initial_____

☐ Foreclosure Info to Tenant

Initial_____

☐ Fire Pits and Fireplace Addendum

Initial_____

☐ Homeowners Association Disclosure

Initial_____

☐ Pool Maintenance Addendum

Initial_____

☐ Bed Bug Addendum

Initial_____

☐ Other:

Initial_____

_____   _____

TENANT 1 DATE   **TENANT 2**

_____

DATE

_____   _____

TENANT 3   **DATE**

AGENT FOR OWNER _____

_____ _____ _____
OWNER DATE   **OWNER**   **DATE**

I HAVE RECEIVED A COPY AND AGREE TO THE TERMS OF THE "TENANT HANDBOOK"

_____
TENANT DATE TENANT DATE

DISCLOSURE OF INFORMATION ON LEAD-BASED PAINT AND LEAD-BASED PAINT HAZARDS

LEAD WARNING STATEMENT

Housing built before 1978 may contain lead-based paint. Lead from paint, paint chips, and dust can pose health hazards if not taken care of properly. Lead exposure is especially harmful to young children and pregnant women. Before renting pre-1978 housing, landlords must disclose the presence of known lead-based paint and lead-based paint hazards in the dwelling. Tenants must also receive a federally approved pamphlet on lead poisoning prevention.

Lessor's Disclosure (initial)

_____(a) Presence of lead-based paint or lead-based paint hazards (check one below):

_____ Known lead-based paint and/or lead-based painting

hazards are present in the housing (explain).

_____

_____

_____ Lessor has no knowledge of lead-based paint and/or lead-based paint hazards in the housing.

_____ (b) Records and reports available to the lessor (check one below):

_____ Lessor has provided the lessee with all available records and reports pertaining to lead-based paint and/or lead-based paint hazards in the housing (list documents below).

_____

_____

_____ Lessor has no reports or record pertaining to lead-based paint and/or lead-based paint hazards in the housing.

Lessee's Acknowledgement (initial)

_____ (a) Lessee has received copies of all information listed above.

_____ (b) Lessee has received the pamphlet Protect Your Family from Lead in Your Home.

Agent's Acknowledgement (initial)

_____ (a) Agent has performed the lessor's obligations under 42 U.S.C. 4852(d) and is aware of his/her responsibility to ensure compliance.

Certification of Accuracy

The following parties have reviewed the information above and certify, to the best of their knowledge, that the information provided by the signatory is true and accurate.

_____   _____
Lessor / Owner Date   Lessor / Owner Date

_____
Lessee Date Lessee Date

_____
Agent of Lessor Date Agent Date

Appendix G
TENANT HANDBOOK©
HOW TO LIVE IN AND CARE FOR THE HOME YOU ARE RENTING

BY PAM KEEN, BROKER

LEARN MORE AT

WWW.PENSACOLAREALTYMASTERS.COM

www.PensacolaRealtyMasters.com

info@pensacolarealtymasters.com

(850) 473-3983 Phone / (850) 473- 3975 Fax

Emergency Cell (850) 512- 6019

CONTENTS

OUR PERSONAL MESSAGE TO YOU

Congratulations on the selection of your new home. Welcome to the Pensacola area and to your new association with Realty Masters of FL located at

4400 Bayou Blvd, Ste #58B, Pensacola, Florida 32503

&

6800 W. Hwy 98, Ste A, Pensacola, Florida 32506

We want to make your association with our firm a pleasant experience and hope you will look to us for all your RENTAL and REAL ESTATE needs.

If you have a home in another part of the USA, we may be able to locate a Property Manager for you through our association with the National Association of Residential Property Managers (NARPM). NARPM is a large association of professional residential property managers, who maintain a high standard of service. If we can help you locate a property manager for your home, please let us know.

Should you decide to purchase a home, call the office and we will help locate a Realtor who is knowledgeable in the area and price range you desire. The home you are renting may also be available to purchase. Please contact this office for more information about the home you are renting.

As Professional Property Managers, we have obligations to both you, as the resident tenant, and to the Owner of the home. This Handbook, **which is part of your lease**, outlines our responsibilities to you and your responsibilities to us and to the home. Please read each paragraph carefully. A good relationship is possible when both parties understand and fulfill each of their responsibilities and obligations.

Clear communication is the key to a successful Landlord/ Tenant relationship. We are always ready to answer questions or to discuss problems.

GENERAL RULES & REGULATIONS

Part of Your Lease - *This Tenant Handbook is part of your lease and is legally binding on both parties.*

The Property- You have leased a home . . . think of it as your own. During the term of this lease, you are in possession of the house and yard. Your obligations are similar to those of the Owner, and you are expected to care for and maintain the premises accordingly.

Rental Payments- All *rents are due and payable, in advance, on the first day of each month*. Monthly bills will not be sent. Payment should be in the form of a check, money order, or certified funds, and made payable to:

Realty Masters of FL

4400 Bayou Blvd, Ste #58B

Pensacola, Florida 32503

Realty Masters of FL

6800 W. Hwy 98, Ste A

Pensacola, Florida 32506

Please mail or deliver your payment to the above address. **WRITE YOUR ADDRESS** on your payment to assure proper credit. All accounting is done by address of the property. Also, to avoid any misunderstanding, please put your address on every correspondence with the office.

You may pay in person, Monday through Friday, 8:30am to 4:30 pm, at 4400 Bayou Blvd, Ste #58, Pensacola, Florida 32503 or 6800 W. Hwy 98, Ste A, Pensacola, Florida 32506. For your after-hour convenience there is a drop box beside the front door to the office. **We do not accept post-dated checks**. Rents remaining unpaid beyond the 3rd day of the month are delinquent and are subject to a late fee. Rents remaining unpaid after the 3rd day of the month may be offered for collection and will be subject to all collection charges and fees incurred. The late fee is 10% + $5 per day. If Realty Masters has to post a 3-day notice on your door you will be charged $20. If Realty Masters mails you a 3-day notice you will be charged $1.

Phone Number- All residents are required to have telephone accessibility and to provide Realty Masters with their home and work phone numbers. Please be sure to notify Realty Masters when you change home or work numbers. Even unlisted numbers must be provided to Realty Masters. You should include your home and work phone numbers with your first rental payment after you move in, or you may send it to us via fax @ 473-3975 or email: christine@ pensacolarealtymasters.com

Returned Checks- The amount of any bad checks, plus the returned check charge allowed by law (5%) must be paid in either certified funds or a money order within 24 hours of notification. Otherwise, legal action may be taken. After a check is returned to us for insufficient funds, you will be required to pay either with a money order or certified funds. If the returned check makes your rent payment late, a late fee will also be due. All amounts due must be paid in full at time of notification.

Default of Rental Payment- *If the rent is not paid by the 3rd of the month, this is your notice that your lease and rental agreement may be canceled after due notice, and that a demand may be made for all monies due*. You will be responsible for all fees, court costs, and legal and collection fees incurred by efforts to collect the rent due. All charges unpaid by the end of the month in which they are charged may be added as additional rent. All remedies and charges for collecting unpaid rent may be used to collect unpaid charges. If rent is paid while a legal action is in process, acceptance of rent will not necessarily stop the legal action.

A separate agreement must be reached if legal action is to be stopped.

<u>Thirty Days Written Notice</u>- Thirty (30) days written notice must be given to Realty Masters before vacating the premises. THE WRITTEN NOTICE IS REQUIRED EVEN IF YOU INTEND TO VACATE AT THE END OF THE LEASE. Also, the Landlord will give you thirty (30) days written notice prior to the end of the lease term if the rental agreement will not be renewed. If Landlord consents to tenant remaining in the premises after the natural expiration of this lease, and no new lease is signed, the tenancy will be extended as a month-to-month tenancy and may be terminated by tenant giving written notice not less than 30 days prior to the end of any monthly payment period or landlord giving written notice not less than 30 days prior to the end of any monthly payment period. **Termination of the tenancy shall occur on the last day of the month**. Notice from the tenant to landlord must be made by certified mail. All other conditions of this lease shall remain in effect. Failure to give above stated notice by tenant prior to end of the lease or any month to month period will result in additional liability of tenant for the following full monthly rental period in addition to security deposit forfeiture. **If tenant fails to vacate after the initial term or any successive consensual periods after the initial term, tenant shall additionally be held liable for holdover (double) rent.** (This does not apply to the military clause)

<u>Breaking Your Lease</u>- The forfeiture of the deposit as a penalty for premature cancellation of the tenancy does

not excuse you from other obligations of your lease. You must leave the premises clean, undamaged and ready for occupancy. Check-in and check-out inspections are required. Tenant is liable for terms of lease including any rents due until property is re-leased in the event of early termination of lease agreement by the Tenant.

Keys and Locks- All locks are not re-keyed with each new resident. One set of keys is issued at the time of possession. Alterations or replacement of locks, installation of bolts, knockers, mirrors or other attachments to the interior or exterior of doors requires the approval of Realty Masters. Realty Masters must have keys to each lock on the house. Realty Masters may gain access and re-key if at any time access is denied, and charge the cost to the Tenant. Copies of the new keys will be available at the office during posted office hours. All keys are to be returned to Realty Masters upon vacating the premises. If you are locked out of your home, you may borrow a key from us Monday through Friday 8:30am to 4:30 pm. There will be a charge for any borrowed key that is not returned within 24 hours.

Trash, Garbage and Recycling- All garbage & trash must be placed in appropriate containers, (Realty Masters does not provide these). All containers are to be discreetly stored. The Tenant is required to make arrangements to have garbage and trash picked up weekly. Containers are not to be out of the storage area except on pick up days. Any recycling items collected must be properly contained and discreetly stored. A total of no more than two 50 gallon trash bags of recyclable materials may be kept on the premises at one time.

Disturbances, Noise and Nuisance- All Tenants, residents and guests are expected to conduct themselves in a way that will not offend or disturb the neighbors or passersby. Any activity that causes extreme or excessive noise, traffic or disturbance of any kind is cause for eviction. This includes loud, lewd music, or vulgar or profane language. If music or other sound can be heard outside the perimeter of the premises leased, it is considered too loud.

Move-In/Move-Out Condition Report- Included in your move-in Package is a Property Condition Report. Realty Masters provides this form so that you can note the condition of the premises, listing all defective items. Please sign your name, date it and return it to Realty Masters with-in 3 days of moving in. A similar report will be used for the move-out condition comparison after vacating the premises. If this report is not returned as outlined under the Florida Residential Landlord and Tenant Act, the property will be assumed to be in acceptable condition and any defects brought to our attention after the 3rd day will be considered your responsibility. No exceptions will be made.

Periodic Surveys- As part of our agreement with Owner of the property, Realty Masters will conduct routine surveys of the condition of the property. You will be notified of any problems, and given 14 days to remedy them. Any breach not corrected will be addressed as per the Florida Residential Landlord and Tenant Act.

Parking/Vehicles- All vehicles shall be parked in assigned areas (garages, parking lots, driveways, parking pads, etc.) Or on the public street where allowed. You are not allowed to park on lawns, sidewalks and other areas not specifically designated for parking. **All vehicles must be registered, licensed and operable at all times**. No vehicle repair (except minor repairs e.g. changing a tire) is allowed at any time. No oil/fluid stains are allowed on the garage floor, driveway, walkways or any other area on the property. If your vehicle leaks fluids, place a protective covering or pan under the vehicle to catch the leaks.

Guests- Any person or persons staying more than three weeks in a three-month period will be considered Tenants, unless prior written permission is obtained from Realty Masters. Only those persons listed on your rental application have permission to occupy the premises. You will be responsible for the behavior of your guests. All portions of this agreement also apply to your guests.

Use of the premises – There shall be no large above ground pools nor trampolines allowed on the premises.

Emergency Maintenance/Repairs- An emergency exists when danger is present or property damage has occurred or is about to occur. Do not abuse the emergency system with other types of calls. To report an emergency, call the emergency phone at 512-6019. Be sure to report the specific emergency and include your telephone number in your message.

If the emergency involves a fire or similar emergency, please notify the proper authorities at 911 before calling our voicemail!!

Insurance- It is highly recommended that you have tenants' insurance. A copy of your declarations page is to be given to management the first month you move in. Please notify your insurance company that Realty Masters of FL is your landlord and must be notified of any change.

Pets- No pets, animals, snakes or birds, etc. of any kind are allowed on the premises unless you have written permission and have paid a pet fee. If permission is given, you will be required to pay a pet fee that will not be refunded. This is for the privilege of having a pet, not for damage. You will be charged for spraying for fleas and/or repair of any damage caused by the pet. You are responsible for your animal at ALL times. Having a pet is a privilege and permission to have the pet on the premises may be revoked at any time without terminating your lease agreement.

WHEN YOU FIRST MOVE IN

Get to Know Your Property- **When you first move-in, locate the breaker** box and note the ground fault circuit breaker (some of these are located by the sinks and not at the breaker box), where the stove, hot water heater and air conditioner breakers are. **Also locate the water shut off for the house.** It usually is in the front yard near the house, often close to a front spigot. If the shut off has been covered over, contact Realty Masters so it can be properly marked. Also, locate the water shut off for the hot water heater and for under the sinks. *Locating these items now may eliminate damage later*. See paragraph III. C. for more information about circuit breakers.

<u>Put this Handbook Where You Can Find it</u>- Keeping it near the phone book works for most people. Before calling Realty Masters, see if the answer to your question is in this handbook. We love hearing from our Tenants, but need to keep our time free for emergencies and urgent matters.

IN AND AROUND THE HOUSE- We live in a warm, moist climate. It is important to keep the vents on the crawl space open, especially in wet weather. Closed vents may cause excessive damage to floor joists and other areas underneath a house. Watch for puddles of water that do not go away around the perimeter of the house. These are often a sign of a water problem underneath. For slab homes, be careful that grass, dirt, flower beds or other coverings do not grow up over the level of the slab. Keep the perimeter of the house clear of all matter. Stack wood away from the exterior walls and off any wooden deck or flooring. Report to Realty Masters any suspected water problems.

<u>Heat/AC Units</u>- All Heat/AC filters need to be changed once a month, and batteries for smoke detectors should be changed at least twice a year. A good rule of thumb is to change your filter and test your battery each month when you pay your electric bill, and to change the battery in your smoke detector each year when the time changes.

Many homes have heat pumps for heating and air conditioning. The air coming from the vents will not be warm in the winter or cool in the summer. Heat pumps are designed for the temperature to be set and then to **leave the control alone**. The air runs over the heating or cooling element, then gradually warms or cools to the desired temperature. During periods of extreme hot or cold temperatures, the heat pump may not keep the house as comfortable as you desire.

When the heat index is high the heat pump may not lower the inside temperature more than about 10 degrees below the outside temperature. Close the window coverings, keep the doors closed, do not run hot appliances (oven, etc.) and take all other precautions given by public authorities. Do not set the thermostat at a low temperature when the outside temperature is over 95 degrees. Poor cooling may also be due to a clogged filter. Check and change the filters monthly.

If water drips from the inside unit, it is usually due to a clogged condensation drain line. Some drains are easy to clean with a vacuum cleaner. If the line becomes clogged, turn off the unit and clear the drain line. If you do not know how, call a heat/AC repair company to get instructions.

Circuit Breakers- Circuit breakers move slightly when triggered. It may appear to be ON when it is has "tripped." To reset, turn the breaker in the OFF position, then back ON again. The ground fault circuit (GFI) breaker detects even slight voltage changes and cuts the power during fluctuations. They are usually used for bathrooms, sink, exterior plugs, garages and some lights. If you lose power to a plug near a water source, it is usually the GFI circuit. Most GFI's located at the breaker box are marked with a red or yellow button. Many homes have the GFI at the plug in outlet. When these "trip," simply reset the breaker as outlined above, or per the instructions on the outlet cover.

Extermination- Please report any pest problem within three (3) days of possession. If not reported in writing, it is agreed that the premises have no infestation of any kind. Any future infestation of any kind, less termites, shall be your responsibility. You are responsible for reporting any suspected or known termite infestation. You are not responsible for termite control. Realty Masters assumes no responsibility for the control of roaches, mice, ants, fleas or other pests. Please notify Realty Masters if you suspect any termite or wood destroying insects around the house or grounds. You will be charged for any damage caused by uncontrolled pests (e.g. ants building nests in the air conditioning unit and damaging the unit.)

Changing Paint, Wallpaper, Etc. - If you want to change the house in any way, please put your proposal in writing and submit it to Realty Masters along with a sample of the paint/wallpaper or drawing (e.g. adding a fence). If approved, you will receive a written confirmation. All tasks must be done in a workmanlike manner, and must be inspected and approved by Realty Masters after completion. Any reimbursements agreed to will occur after approval.

MAINTENANCE, DAMAGE AND REPAIR- You are expected to maintain the home and keep it in as good a condition as when you took possession. Only repairs required because of normal wear will be made by Realty Masters. You will be charged for repairs caused by misuse or neglect.

Put Maintenance Requests in Writing- Maintenance Request Forms are in your Rental Package. Put all routine requests in writing, using this form. Be specific about the problem (e.g. RIGHT-the right burner on the stove does not work; WRONG-the stove isn't working). Write clearly and legibly. If you are not contacted by a repair person within 48 hours (not including weekends or holidays) after reporting a problem, please notify Realty Masters so the call can be reassigned. You may fax your requests to us at 473-3975 or email fern@pensacolarealtymasters.com.

Who Does What- All "breakdowns," system failures and structural defects must be reported to Realty Masters immediately. If an urgent repair is needed (i.e. hot water heater leaking) YOU are responsible for stopping further damage from occurring, if possible. If there is a leak, stop the water source immediately. If the problem is electrical, turn off the breaker serving that appliance or area until the repairman arrives. Realty Masters will make any necessary repairs within a reasonable time. You will not be reimbursed for any unauthorized repairs you make.

Some examples of maintenance you are expected to do at your own expense:

Replace light bulbs

Torn or damaged screens

Replace or repair cabinet catches, knobs or handles

Replace heater/air-conditioner filters EVERY MONTH

Relight gas furnace or hot water heaters

Treat for fire ants and other lawn pests

Keep flower beds weeded and edged and add fresh bedding once a year

Replace batteries in smoke detectors (please notify Realty Masters if smoke detector is inoperable)

Phone jacks and cable outlets if desired.

Minor plumbing

Examples of repairs management will make at no expense to you:

Repairs to heater/air-conditioning systems from normal use

Replace heating units for hot water tanks from normal use

Repair leaks in roof

Major plumbing

Remove broken electrical components

Repair/paint rotted wood (please notify management if noted)

Treat for termites

Examples of repairs for which you will be held responsible:

Replace heating elements/hot water tanks if caused by empty tank

Repairing burst water pipes when caused by freezing weather

Any unusual damage or extraordinary wear on any of the floors, walls, ceilings, caused by pets, animals, children, guests, smoking or any unusual or unreasonable use

Damage to fences, outside walls, shrubbery, trees or plantings

Unauthorized Repairs- Please do not make any repairs or authorize any maintenance without written permission from Realty Masters. All repairs must be authorized by us. Except as provided in the Florida Residential Landlord and Tenant Act, rent cannot be withheld because of needed repairs nor can the cost of needed repairs be deducted from the rent.

Lawns and Grounds-You are expected to care for the lawn and grounds, keeping them in as good condition as when you took possession. This care includes regularly cutting the grass; fertilizing the lawn; trimming shrubs; edging all walkways; curbs and driveways; treating fire ant beds; cleaning the roof and gutters of leaves, debris, and pine needles and keeping vines from growing onto the house. Please keep shrub and tree growth away from the roof, eaves, and sides of the house. You are required to report any condition which can cause damage, permanent or temporary, to the grounds and to treat for lawn pests. Flowering trees must be pruned at the proper time of the year for their species and all flowerbeds must be kept free of weeds, grass, etc. Whatever is in the beds as a cover (pine straw, pine bark, etc.) must be maintained by the Tenant. Do not leave hoses connected to exterior faucets with the water turned on.

Light Bulbs- At move-in, all light fixtures will be equipped with the proper light bulbs. All burned out light bulbs are to be replaced during the Tenant's occupancy (including floodlights). Upon moving out, all lights must be equipped with the proper number and kind of bulbs. For decorative bulbs, all must match. Light bulbs must be 60 watts unless otherwise specified on the lighting fixture.

Plumbing/Septic Systems - You are responsible for keeping all sinks, lavatories and commodes open. Please do not allow anyone to throw anything into the plumbing system or to use it for any purpose other than for what it is designed. You will be responsible for any damage or stoppage after five (5) days of occupancy unless it was caused by mechanical failure of the plumbing system.

<u>Waterbeds</u>- You will be responsible for ANY damage caused by a waterbed. Waterbed insurance is available.

<u>Walls and Ceilings</u>- Please keep the walls of the home clean and unmarred. Do not paint or wallpaper the walls without *prior written approval* of Realty Masters. You are welcome to hang pictures on the walls as long as the walls are clean and unmarred when you move out. All walls, baseboards and trim must be washed before vacating. All ceilings must be dusted/vacuumed regularly and before vacating. NO SMOKING IS ALLOWED INSIDE OF THE HOME AT ANY TIME.

<u>Vinyl Floor Coverings/Hardwood Floors</u>- Vinyl and hardwood floors must be washed with a solution of warm water and soap. A thorough cleaning is necessary three or four times a year. Do not use gas, benzine, naphtha, turpentine, or waxes containing these solvents. Rubber heel marks can easily be removed with the proper product. Do not apply varnish, lacquer or shellac to the floor. When waxing, use a water-emulsion, self-polishing types of wax such as Johnson's Vinyl Wax for vinyl and Johnson's Paste Wax for hardwood floors. Do not use any solvent based waxes. You will be responsible for damage done by using improper cleaning materials. (You are also responsible for damage to flooring such as broken tiles or torn floor covering or improper cleaning procedures.)

Carpet Care- Routine carpet care requires a thorough vacuuming at least <u>once a week</u> to remove the soil from the carpet and to keep the pile erect. Heavy traffic areas require more frequent vacuuming to eliminate the course particles that can act as an abrasive on the fiber. You must have a motor driven brush-and-beater type vacuum cleaner if the home you rent has carpet. Shampooing is usually required about once a year and is your responsibility. Before moving in, the carpets are professionally cleaned and you must have them <u>professionally</u> cleaned upon vacating. A copy of the cleaning company's receipt is required at the time of check-out. Please check with Realty Masters before moving out for recommended carpet cleaning companies.

Stoves- If the oven or broiler will not operate check the timer on the stove. Generally, the knob will pop out if the timer is off. Turn the knob until it pops out. Instructions for other types are on the face of the stove. Be careful when cleaning the oven that oven cleaner does not drip onto the cabinets below or onto the floor. Do not use oven cleaner on self-cleaning or continuous cleaning ovens. You will be charged for damage to an appliance caused by improper use or cleaning, or by lack of maintenance.

Dishwashers- Use at least once a week. Seals may dry and the motor may be damaged by long periods of not being run. Clean the door and check the bottom of the dishwasher each use for items that may fall from the racks. Check the perimeter of the door for food items falling from the counter.

Garbage Disposals- Garbage disposals are not for bones, greasy items, meat, or any other similar materials. If the motor buzzes, turn the switch off. Unjam the disposal by turning the blade backwards with a broom handle or a wrench. Reset the circuit breaker on the bottom or the side of the disposal (this is usually a small red or yellow button). If the unit turns easily with a wrench but not with power, call for service. Almost all disposal jams are from what is put into them or misuse.

Washer/Dryer Hookups- When you install your washer and dryer, it is a good time to check your hoses and washers to eliminate leaks. If you are going to be absent from the property for an extended period of time, turn off the hot and cold water supply. Check the wall and floor monthly for evidence of a hidden leak.

CLEANING AND HOW TO'S- We work hard to deliver to you a clean, well maintained and comfortable home with all the mechanical equipment operating properly. Proper cleaning and maintenance will keep the home and its equipment safe and usable for you. The key to proper cleaning is to do it often. Set up a weekly schedule. Monitor the work and ensure that cleaning is performed as often as needed. A properly maintained home is a team effort involving the Owner who keeps structural and mechanical maintenance up-to-date; the Property Manager who keeps a record of necessary maintenance and places responsible people in the property; and the Tenant who keeps the property clean, performs cosmetic maintenance and promptly reports any structural or mechanical failure to Management.

Minimum Cleaning Standards-

Keep windows and storm doors clean, inside and outside; interior cleaning at least once a month, exterior cleaning every six months. Wash between windows and screens quarterly.

Wash interior doors, doorways and walls in heavily traveled areas every 1-2 months.

Clean dust, dirt and debris from the upper and lower sliding glass door tracks monthly.

Clean stove, drip pans, under drip pans, oven racks and drawer, broiler pan, hood, filter and vent biweekly.

Mop and wax vinyl floors biweekly.

Dust baseboards, window sills, window grids, tops of windows, ceiling fans, doors, ceilings and corners of the room monthly.

Clean heater/air conditioner air return grate and change filter each month. (A good rule is when you pay your power bill, change your filter).

Clean and sweep out fireplace. Clean fireplace grate, screen and glass.

Replace burned-out light bulbs as needed, clean lighting fixtures as needed.

Curtains and blinds, if provided, should be cleaned or washed semiannually.

Bathrooms should be cleaned weekly. This includes toilet bowls and base, sink, mirror, floor, bathtub and shower (including walls). Wipe out medicine cabinet, drawers and cabinets.

Caulk tub as necessary.

Sweep out garage as needed.

Counter tops and Cabinets- Always use cutting boards and hot pads when chopping, cutting or placing hot items on counter tops. Do not use abrasive cleaners on counter tops as they will scratch. All unpainted cabinets need to be cleaned regularly with a wood cleaner (such as Murphy's Oil Soap) and treated with a wood preserver (such as Scott's Liquid Gold). All cabinets must be vacuumed out and the drawer/door fronts cleaned as above before vacating.

Kitchen Appliances- Each kitchen appliance must be cleaned regularly: in particular, the stove hood, the filter in the stove hood, the oven, under the burners on the stove and the drip pans. Please do not put aluminum foil on the drip pans. Upon moving out, all drip pans must be new. Please clean under the refrigerator, washer, and dryer regularly. Not cleaning all these items regularly can cause excessive wear and tear, for which you will be responsible.

<u>Fireplaces</u>- If there is a fireplace in your home, please do not burn pine or any other "sappy" wood. This causes a buildup of residue in the chimney and increases the possibility of fire. The fireplace is not a place to burn cardboard, Holiday wrappings, pine needles, etc. Chimneys should be professionally cleaned every two years.

MOVING OUT

<u>Put It in Writing</u>- Before notice to vacate is accepted by Realty Masters, it MUST be put in writing. The notice must include the date you anticipate having the property ready for your move-out survey and where you are moving to (even if you don't have a forwarding address, list the city and state where you will be relocating). **Notice must be received by Realty Masters *at least thirty (30) days* before you move out**. Also, the Landlord will give you thirty (30) days written notice prior to the end of the lease term if the rental agreement will not be renewed.

<u>Marketing During the Notice Period</u>- After you have given notice that you intend to move, the property may be listed for sale or rent. The most probable showing hours are between 9:00am and 6:00pm. The property must be available and in good condition during the market time. Illness and children's birthday parties are acceptable reasons for rescheduling a showing. Inconvenience, out of town guests, and no one home are not acceptable reasons to reschedule. You will be called prior to showing. If there is no answer or no answering system, the call is still considered notice. If permission is given, we will call your work number. A call to

your place of residence is the usual and customary practice in the Pensacola area, and is considered notice. Extra effort on your part is expected in keeping the house and yard neat and clean during marketing. Minimum showing condition:

All beds made and rooms neat

Floors are recently vacuumed; clutter free, especially no piles of dirty clothes

Kitchen and baths are clean, sinks are clean and empty

Walls are clean and unmarred

Dogs are out of the way, litter boxes are clean and odor free

TV is off or volume turned low so as not to be intrusive

Yard is mowed, trimmed and in good condition

Blinds/curtains are open and home is well lit (when possible)

The better a home shows, the more likely it will rent or sell quickly. The faster a new resident is found, the less you will be bothered by showings. A home that shows well benefits everyone!

The Move-Out/Check out Condition Survey- ***Keys and professional carpet cleaning receipts must be turned in to*** *the office before an inspection will be done. Inspections are done after keys and receipts have been turned in and* <u>*without tenants being present*</u>*.* Move in and move out inspection reports will be compared and used to determine damages, if any, along with pictures of the move out inspection.

All utilities are to be left on for three days after your scheduled inspection/ move out date.

Surveys are made only after you have completely vacated the premise, the premises are cleaned, carpets are professionally cleaned and dry (receipt required, chemical dry cleaning is unacceptable), the yard is mowed and edged, all trash hauled off, shrubs trimmed, flower beds have fresh bedding, and you have turned over the keys and professional carpet cleaning receipt to the office. A room-by-room check will be made, including interior, exterior, grounds, appliances, windows, curtains, blinds, etc.

Appendix D provides some of the cleaning guidelines. Upon receipt of your written notice to vacate, another copy will be sent to you. *Most Tenants who use the guidelines pass the survey on the first appointment.*

A reinspection fee (minimum, $35.00) will be charged for each return trip that is required after the first inspection should the inspector need to go back for any reason.

<u>Breaking the Lease</u>- If you should break your lease you will be responsible for all costs incurred in securing a new Tenant. We work diligently to reduce your costs should you break your lease. If you find you have to move before the end of your lease, we will market the property promptly. You must pay a full months rent for every month until a new Tenant is secured. When the new Tenant moves in, your obligation ceases. Forfeiture of your security deposit does not excuse you from other obligations of the lease. You must follow all procedures for marketing, cleaning and check-out.

Following is a list of the most common charges for breaking a lease. These are some, but not all of the possible charges:

A re-leasing and/or breaking lease fee

Rent until the new lease takes effect.

Lawn maintenance (you need to arrange for that before leaving)

Utilities (keep them on in your name until notified of a new Tenant)

Advertising

Forfeiture of Security Deposit

Return of the Security Deposit- THE SECURITY DEPOSIT MAY NOT BE USED AS THE LAST MONTH'S RENT!!!!

The security deposit will be refunded in accordance with Florida Statutes §83.49, which, in summary, provides that upon the vacating of the premises for termination of the lease, if the landlord does not intend to impose a claim on the security deposit, the landlord shall have 15 days to return the security deposit, otherwise the landlord shall have 30 days to give the tenant written notice of the landlord's intention to impose a claim on the deposit and the reason for imposing the claim. Unless the tenant objects to the imposition of the landlord's claim or the amount thereof within 15 days after receipt of the landlord's notice of intention to impose a claim, the landlord may then deduct the amount of his or her claim and shall remit the balance of the deposit to the tenant within 30 days after the date of the notice of intention to impose a claim.

Following are the requirements for a full refund;

Have given thirty (30) days written notice prior to vacating.

Have left the premises clean and undamaged and followed the check out procedures.

Have left all walls clean and unmarred. (Homes are NOT painted between each Tenant)

Have paid all charges and rents due.

Have removed all debris, rubbish, and discarded all items from the premises.

Have provided a forwarding street address and a telephone number. No P.O. Boxes are accepted as a forwarding address.

Have an acceptable move-out/check-out condition survey report by the Property Manager or Inspector.

GENERAL – ALL AREAS

__Windows, windowsills, sash & frames are clean

__Blinds are all thoroughly washed

__Base boards, molding, and trim washed down

__Ceiling free of cobwebs

__Walls and doors wiped & washed down

__Sliding door tracks free of dirt

__All vents & air conditioner registers cleaned

__Outlets and switch plate covers cleaned

__Carpets vacuumed

__All vinyl/ tile/ wood surfaces swept & mopped

__All nail holes & dents on wall are filled & smooth. Fill must match wall color or you must paint the entire wall!

__ Strip and wax stained VCT Tiled floors

__ Replace all smoke & CO2 detector batteries

__All burnt out light bulbs replaced throughout with 60 watt bulbs unless otherwise stated

NOTE: Carpets MUST be professionally cleaned and a receipt must be provided to management.

KITCHEN

__ Cupboards and drawers emptied and cleaned

__ Outside of cabinets cleaned with mild soap

__ Finish wood cabinets with Scotts Liquid Gold

__ Fridge & freezer emptied & cleaned with white vinegar including trays, shelves, seal, handle

__ Top and outside of fridge/freezer cleaned

__ Fridge/freezer pulled out and floor cleaned underneath

__ Stove cleaned including outside, inside, underneath, around & racks/ drawers

__ Stove drip pans cleaned or replaced

__ Stove hood vent cleaned or replaced

__ Sink scoured and caulked if necessary

__ Floor and baseboards scrubbed

__ All surface areas cleaned

__ Dishwasher surfaces cleaned

LIVING ROOM/ HALLWAYS/ BEDROOMS

__ Air conditioner filter, grate & cover clean

__Thermostat set to 78 in summer/ 68 in winter

__ Clean & sweep out fireplace & screen

__ Heat vents and registers wiped off

__ Baseboards cleaned

BATHROOMS

__ Exhaust fans cleaned

__ Medicine cabinets emptied and cleaned

__ Toilet tank, seat, and base cleaned

__ Toilet bowl scrubbed

__ Floor and baseboards scrubbed

__ Sink cleaned

__ Shower curtain removed

__ Outlets and switch plate covers cleaned

__ Vanity surface and under vanity cleaned

__ Mirror cleaned

__ Tub/ Shower floor and walls scrubbed (free of soap scum and mildew)

__ Tub/ Shower and around countertops caulked

LAWN

__ PETS: Remove all pet droppings and dispose

__ Mow lawn and pick up any trash

__ Walkways & driveways swept & edged

__ Rake all leaves on premises & bag

__ Trim all hedges & shrubs below 4 feet

__ Remove weeds from fence, house & beds

__ Replace flower beds with fresh bedding

GARAGE/ PATIOS/ DECKS/ STORAGE

__ Empty and clean out storage and/or garage

__ Sweep ceilings and walls for cobwebs

__ Sweep and mop floors

__ Remove any stored items from attic

EXTERIOR

__ All exterior doors washed

__ Wash all windows and rinse screens

__ Wash mailbox and post with soap

__ All screens secured on windows

__ All doors and windows are locked

__ All trash and belongings are removed from the home and the yard!

NOTE: Trash companies will NOT pick up boxes, furniture, etc. left by the curb or anything that does not fit inside trash cans. You MUST call ECUA to schedule pick up or arrange haul to dump or you will be charged a minimum of $50 for trash removal.

__ Baseboards cleaned

__Carpets vacuumed

EMERGENCY/DISASTER PROCEDURES

A and B - These are the procedures, plans and responsibilities for emergency/disaster related situations. Please read each of them carefully and regularly review them, especially during the summer months. Since a Hurricane is the natural disaster most likely to happen in our area, special emphasis has been placed on hurricane preparedness.

Make Your Plan Now- The key to safely and properly handling any emergency/disaster is pre-planning and staying calm during and after the event. Being prepared is every individual's responsibility. Don't rely only on the authorities. Take charge and plan now so you can be better prepared to take action when the time comes. Advanced planning allows for fewer mistakes and greater safety for you, your family, and the home you are caring for. It is easy to forget even little things in the anxiety, which often comes with an emergency. To avoid unnecessary stress, get ready now. As Pensacola Mayor, Joseph P. Riley Jr. says, "No one ever got hurt or killed because they were overprepared."

Two Types of Emergency-
The first type is one that is specific to the property you rent (i.e. a tree falls on this house, or the hot water heater bursts). Part A addresses this Non-Disaster Emergency.

The second type of emergency is an area wide disaster (i.e. a hurricane or tornado) Appendix B addresses this type of emergency procedure.

Because we get advance warning for a hurricane, many people choose to leave town. If you leave, you still must secure the property prior to leaving. Then complete

Appendix C, fax or bring it to the office before leaving. If the disaster does occur, please call before coming back to the property.

<u>What You Do</u>- Everything an Owner would do to protect the property, you are expected to do. The first priority is to stop additional damage. Review Section II. A. regularly. We have many thunder and lightening storms, power outages and high winds. An emergency could happen at any time. Be prepared.

A. NON-DISASTER EMERGENCY PROCEDURES

(i.e. Kitchen fire, hot water heater burst, burst water pipe, tree falls on house, etc.)

<u>Upon first occurrence or discovery of problem, secure from further damage immediately</u>. Following is a summary of what to expect. Please post this note in a visible place. If any of these actions do not occur, notify the office immediately. Keeping everyone on schedule is a cooperative effort, and you are part of the team.

Resident Responsibility

- Take steps to prevent additional damage immediately

- Turn off the source of water or electricity or gas, as the situation demands

- Notify Realty Masters! If it is after hours, use emergency line at (850) 512-6019.

- Make claim on Renters insurance and notify property manager of insurance coverage

- Provides emergency (police, fire, etc.) report to Realty Masters within 5 days of the incident

- Provide access for insurance, repair people, etc. to assess and repair damage

- Notify management of delays, "no show" appointments, problems with repairs

Realty Masters Responsibility-

- Notifies the Owner, insurance company and repair companies

- Takes pictures of damage for Owner report

- Obtains estimates and facilitates repairs

- Inspects and takes pictures of finished work

You will be contacted within 48 hours by the insurance company. They will assess the damage. Within 3-10 days, depending on the severity of the damage, the repairs will begin. Please remember that work is performed during normal daytime business hours, Monday through Friday and may require several days to complete. The repair company will set a time with you to work on the house. If you desire, they can check out a key from the office. You will need to call the office to coordinate with the office manager for key check-outs.

After the repairs are complete, management should call you to set up a time to re-inspect. If there is a delay, please contact the office. Sometimes the repair company is not prompt in scheduling the inspection. Your help is vital to this process. You are responsible for any loss to the Owner due to Resident negligence. If the damage was caused by a resident or a guest, please be aware all charges not covered by insurance will be billed to you.

B. DISASTER EMERGENCY PROCEDURES

1. Have an emergency preparedness plan, a checklist and a storm kit.

2. Upon first notification that a disaster emergency may occur, if you plan on leaving the property, please call the office and leave us a message on the voicemail with an additional contact for you. —OR-

3. Fax or deliver the same message to the office of Realty Masters of FL (fax 473-3975)

4. Stay tuned to the local news media and follow all recommended precautions and instructions.

5. During the storm or before leaving, please be sure to:

    1. Turn off main breaker to house

    2. Turn off main gas line to house (Call gas company for instructions)

    3. Turn off main water supply to house

    4. Take all recommended precautions by the local news media and storm bulletins

    5. Secure your pets, inside. If it not safe for you outside, it is not safe for your pets either!

6. Secure all outside items including bringing in swing sets, play houses, small planters, anything that could turn into a flying object during high winds

7. Secure house against damage

8. Make sure management has a key for your house (have you changed locks lately?)

9. If you are leaving town, call the office before leaving and before returning to verify that the house is safe to return to.

YOU ARE RESPONSIBLE FOR SECURING THE HOME AGAINST POSSIBLE DAMAGE. EVERYTHING A HOMEOWNER SHOULD DO, YOU ARE EXPECTED TO DO.

SUMMARY

This Handbook Is For You- In the excitement of moving, we often don't remember all the instructions and requirements of the lease. This handbook was written to be used as a reference for you. Place it where you can easily find it. Before calling the office, look to see if the answer you seek is here. If you find something you think would be helpful to others, but is not included, please notify your Property Manager. We are always looking for additional ways to serve you.

Welcome to Realty Masters- Again, welcome to our area and your new home. Please take advantage of the many opportunities to enjoy the beautiful and friendly Pensacola area. Should you decide to make this your permanent home, call the office. We would be happy to help you find a home to purchase.

Appendix H
List and Location of Key Charts